HYPERINFLATION
OR
DEPRESSION?

HYPERINFLATION
OR
DEPRESSION?

Richard G. Zambell

WEISS RESEARCH, INC.
2000 Palm Beach Lakes Boulevard • Suite 200
West Palm Beach, Florida 33409

Library of Congress Cataloging in Publication Data

Zambell, Richard G., 1952-
Hyperinflation or depression?

Bibliography: p.

1. United States—Economic conditions—1981-
2. Inflation (Finance)—United States
3. Long Waves (Economics)—United States
I. Title.
HC106.8.Z35   1984   338.5'443'0973   84-7296
ISBN 0-9613048-3-9

Acknowledgements: Martin D. Weiss for editing.

Contents

Introduction

Throughout the past decades, we have assumed we could manipulate economic growth in any desired direction. But history has proven us wrong.

No President, Congressional representative, Senator, Federal Reserve Board member, or common citizen has wanted high interest rates, rapid inflation, out-of-control budget deficits or increasingly severe recessions—let alone an unemployment rate now stuck close to double-digit levels. But despite everyone's desire to avoid these events and steer the economy towards a golden era, they still occurred and continue to plague the U.S. economy.

No matter what policy actions were attempted—wage/price controls, wage/price guidelines, floating or fixed foreign exchange rates, selective credit controls, supply-side economics, rapid defense buildups, tax cuts or increases, tight or easy monetary policy—no one has been able to generate sustained economic growth with low interest rates, low inflation, and low unemployment. What then is really going on in the U.S. economy?

These failures have led most Americans to modify their

views of how successful the Government can be in altering the economy. If a Presidential candidate told you he had a guaranteed plan to prevent all future recessions, you would probably scoff, realizing that recessions occur about every 3-5 years to correct the imbalances that inevitably develop during an economic growth period—excessive inflation, debts, business inventories, etc.; and that recessions are necessary evils to clean up the economic system, setting a solid foundation for the next economic expansion.

Since U.S. policymakers have never demonstrated an ability to prevent a recession as they would surely like, then why is it presumed they can prevent a depression? Why is it generally assumed the 1930s depression was somehow a policy error that should have been prevented? History indicates just the opposite. The U.S. and other world economies have experienced depressions approximately every 40-60 years as an inevitable process to correct the massive excesses that develop over a long period of growth.

The same basic problems that lead to recessions also lead to depressions but on a much larger scale. Debts become so pervasive that debtors are unable to cover payments with their current income flows, resulting in huge loan defaults and national debt repudiations. Companies and banks fail at record rates. And, ironically, speculative markets soar in anticipation of an inflationary surge which is believed will result from desperate Government actions to promote a rapid economic recovery. But as the Federal Reserve slows the flow of money into the economy to prevent that very price explosion, the speculative bubble bursts, causing society's wealth and spending power to plunge.

The past four-year period has not really been "abnormal" as many currently believe. Rather it conforms very closely to what happens in the latter stages of a long-wave cycle—a 40-60 year period which eventually ends in depression. Nor is the often cited "unprecedented level" of real, or inflation-adjusted, interest rates an unheard of situation. In fact, the two phenomena are closely related; a major reason for the eventual collapse is the need to maintain high, inflation-adjusted interest rates to prevent a price acceleration. Looking back in history, high real interest rates occurred in the 1820s, 1870s, and 1920s-30s—periods leading to or during depressions. Therefore, when people cite today's high real interest rates as being unprecedented, they are erroneously only looking at the postwar period.

It is now time for the electorate and policy officials to realize the economy cannot be completely and permanently redirected towards such noble goals as strong economic growth, low interest rates, low inflation, and low unemployment without incurring considerable pain and suffering. There are periods during the 40-60 year long-wave cycle during which such ideal conditions will temporarily and naturally develop. But the economy is dynamic; it changes. And the policies that worked in that stable or golden period will not yield the same results later in the long wave.

The imbalances that develop during the cycle increasingly dictate the painful path that must be followed to erase those problems or stumbling blocks. Only after a successful cleansing period, typically requiring 10-20 years, can a strong base once again be established for the next upward phase of the long wave. Before a period of prosperity can again be experienced, however, the U.S. must first incur the 1980s depression.

Two earlier books discuss the mathematical techniques and economic theory that are the basis for the following forecasts and recommendations. From my *Linked Weekly, Monthly, Quarterly Econometric Models of the U.S. Economy (Volume 1)* and *Condensed Weekly, Monthly, Quarterly Econometric Models of the U.S. Economy (Volume 2)*, the typically competing Keynesian, monetarist, and supply-side economic theories are synthesized whereby each has its own time and place during the 40-60 year economic cycle.

1

An Overview—the Causes and Consequences of a 1980s Depression

The past four-year period of economic turmoil—the worst cumulative economic performance since the 1930s—is the prelude to the 1980s depression. We had recessions in three of the past four years, whereas in the past a 9-12 month recession occurred every 3-5 years. Now every year of recovery is overwhelmed by 3-4 years of recession.

As a result, the 1982 and 1983 unemployment rates averaged 9.7%, a level last observed when we were recovering from the Great Depression. Corporations have closed their doors at a speed unparalleled since the worst of the 1930s. And even though interest rates are down sharply from their 1980-1981 peaks, they are still historically high. Most important, real or inflation adjusted interest rates are at their highest level since the 1930s, stifling economic activity in an almost insidious way, much akin to slow strangulation.

The cause of our strong economic activity in the 1950s-1970s period was the rapid money infusion by the Federal Reserve. However, this seed money led to a crop of excessive bad debts, highly imbedded inflationary fears, and historically high actual inflation. Subsequently, as U.S. inflation soared to double-digit rates in 1980 and 1981, the Federal Reserve started to limit the amount of money being supplied to the U.S. (and indirectly to the world) economy in an effort to first stop inflation's acceleration and to secondly cause an actual deceleration over several years. Although there have been spurts of excessive money creation since 1979, by and large, the period marks the beginning of a deflationary policy.

The direct result of this money slowdown, however, is economic stagnation, along with domestic and international financial disorder as individuals, businesses, and nations find it increasingly difficult to repay their debts, stretching out loans and defaulting on interest payments. In mid-1982 an international financial collapse almost occurred as Mexico nearly defaulted on debt payments—an event which would have set off a chain reaction of other national defaults and bank failures. But a catastrophe was avoided by a massive and unprecedented bail-out effort by the Federal Reserve from mid-1982 to mid-1983 as they pumped as much money into the U.S. and worldwide economies as was necessary to stabilize the financial arena.

This fresh money, in turn, fueled the sharpest stock market rally during a 12-month period in U.S. history—even exceeding the great surge in 1927-1929. The stock market gains and the sharp money rise itself were two very powerful catalysts for strong economic growth in 1983.

But such booms cannot last forever. The money infusion or Fed bail-out necessary to keep it going can take place only once; it cannot be repeated without incurring the heavy cost of a rapid resurgence in inflation. It is for this reason the Federal Reserve once again began to slow money growth sharply in 1983's second half. The natural consequences should be a recession that arrives sooner than history typically dictates.

We are caught in a Catch-22 gridlock. To avoid an international financial collapse and depression, strong economic activity must be spurred by explosive money growth. Yet it is this very money growth that quickly leads to an inflation resurgence which the Federal Reserve then must counter by cutting off those money flows, resulting in yet another recession, further intensifying the debt crisis and precipitating more failures—an inevitable vicious circle.

Ironically, the international debt problem and our massive business failures in recent years are a direct result of the inflation slowdown itself. Because of slower inflation, the market does not allow businesses to raise product prices to cover their high fixed costs. And, even worse, their expensive production facilities have turned into excess capacity due to the slowing worldwide economy.

Over the past several years, not only have businesses overexpanded at the wrong time and bought artificially high priced plant, equipment, and inventories, they have compounded their problems by purchasing such items on credit at outrageously high interest rates. But, these sins are ones which individuals and nations also share. Because of much slower inflation, interest payments now become much more burdensome, especially in light of the extremely disappointing pay increases for individuals, downward-revised revenue forecasts of corporations, and exploding budget and trade deficits of Governments.

The money and debt creation that led to high growth in the 1960s is now being restricted, cutting off the life-blood to the worldwide economy. As the number of defaults rises, lenders obviously cease lending to anyone who may have difficulty in repaying. Business failures increase dramatically as a result, particularly with each new recession. And the Federal Reserve, the guardian of how much money flows directly into the U.S. economy, is restricting this money flow to hold onto recently hard-fought gains in cutting underlying double-digit inflation of 1980-1981 in half.

The fact that it has taken all these drastic actions over the past half decade to reduce inflation is a symptom of something truly wrong. And yet, the slower inflation has itself set off a chain reaction leading to worldwide depression. The world economy, much like a drug addict, is starved for ever larger doses of money and suffers withdrawal pains even with the slightest reduction or interruption.

A logical question is: Why the zeal to control inflation if international financial collapse and depression are the end results of a successful campaign?

First, most policymakers have finally begun to realize that there is no such thing as "a little inflation." They now are beginning to recognize that, once the reflation process begins, it takes more and more money to achieve the same economic growth. But this extra money pumping leads to accelerating inflation with about a 1½ year time lag. Initially the economic goals are met. However, the inflationary cost of that achievement is not incurred until later. If several consecutive years of rapid money infusion occur, inflationary periods begin to overlap — i.e. double up and triple up—developing into hyperinflation or a rate of inflation so high relative to the nation's historical past that a political mandate develops to stop it.

At this stage, policymakers are more concerned with the consequences of accelerating inflation than the consequences of recession. Interest rates surge to unbelievable heights. Businesses, unsure of the future rewards relative to high upfront costs, stop investing in new plant and equipment. In other words, rapid inflation breeds uncertainty and uncertainty itself precipitates a natural correction. It is this burst in the speculative bubble which then acts much like a political mandate to bring the inflation binge under control, thereby supporting the Federal Reserve's credit restraining actions. In response to the unavailability of credit, individuals, corporations, and nations reduce their spending, which helps lower the inflation rate with a lag. There really is no choice in the matter. The natural flow of economic events triggers mechanisms which bring inflation under control through a cessation of spending.

The key, however, is this: As long as inflation was low in the 1950s and 1960s, the recessions needed to reduce it were far less severe while, at the same time, there was no pressing national desire to go all the way in order to slow inflation beyond the previous low point and keep it there. But later, as greater and greater inflationary pressures became lodged in the system, bigger and longer recessions were necessary to achieve the same success in preventing an uncontrollable inflation acceleration. Eventually, a depression develops as the only natural recourse to finally resolve the problem.

Many analysts feel inflation is unavoidable. However, history demonstrates that to pursue the inflationary path takes a conscious effort which is often not feasible either financially or politically. Under normal circumstances individuals, corporations, and Government institutions are all pushed very forcibly on a course to control inflation. In England, for example, even though an economic depression is being incurred under the Thatcher Administration (with a 13%+ unemployment rate in 1983 versus 5.0% in 1981), the public is supportive. The electorate has seen too many years of the insidious damage caused by rampaging inflation. Even though the costs are high, the British apparently perceive the costs of not succeeding to be even higher.

What is the cost of not preventing hyperinflation with a depression? The most compelling one is that a nation's political institutions never survive it without radical change. The middle class—the usual support for any Government—sees all its wealth destroyed. In contrast, while a depression is a calamity, 70%+ of the labor force continues to work productively, and the middle class, although damaged, remains largely intact as a social and political force.

Without this middle-class base the political process collapses: The French hyperinflation of the 1780s-1790s overturning the rule of traditional French leadership and bringing the warring Napoleon to power; the German hyperinflation of 1922-1923 toppling the Weimar administration and bringing Hitler to power; and the continual hyperinflation of Italy and South America, leading to frequent political chaos, are all typical examples. But once again, the irony of this other road is that it does not avoid the inevitable depression even for all the turmoil that results. All hyperinflations burn themselves out eventually, degenerating into depressions after all.

Money Growth Sets the Pace

What governs short-run and long-run changes in the economy? The two most critical factors in the short-run are money growth and stock market movements.

Money, as measured by "M-1," is the most potent factor. If we have rapid money growth today, we can generally expect to see rapid economic activity 4-6 months hence. Conversely, if we get a sharp deceleration in the Fed's money provisioning, we will probably face a recession also about 4-6 months from now. Based on this alone, you might think the solution to all our troubles is to simply provide the economy with more and more money to ensure rapid economic growth and produce a low unemployment rate.

Unfortunately, however, money growth has a longer-term negative side effect that is even more powerful than its short-run positive impact; there is also a very close relationship between rapid money growth today and inflation about 1½ years later. For example, the double-digit inflation of the early 1980s was a direct result of the money explosion that occurred from 1977 to 1979. On the other hand, since late 1979, the Federal Reserve has made an about face, ending the 1977-1979 acceleration and at times even slowing money growth dramatically, although in a somewhat irregular way. The initial result was the recessions of 1980 and 1981-1982. But the longer-term consequence has been a sharp drop in the inflation rate by 1982. Consumer price inflation rose from 4.5% in early 1976 to nearly 14% in early 1981, followed by a drop to 2.5% in mid-1983, and it was primarily the Fed's on-and-then-off money pumping that caused these inflation cycles.

The radical contrast between money's initial positive and

later negative effects is the underlying basis for the Government's inherent policy dilemma regarding the unemployment rate and inflation. Because of these relationships, no politician or economist can promise perpetual rapid economic growth, sustained low interest rates, a continued low unemployment rate, and an everlasting mild inflation. They are contradictory goals.

The Role of the Stock Market

The second most critical factor affecting the economy in the short run is the stock market. Many just tend to view stocks as legalized gambling or, at best, a risky investment. But the stock market significantly impacts economic activity. Aside from being a source of funds for businesses through new stock flotations, by far the stock market's greatest influence is on consumer wealth which, in turn, is a key factor in determining their ability to buy goods and services. On average, movements in total wealth impact overall consumer spending about two quarters later. So a surge in consumer wealth in the second quarter, for example, should boost consumer spending significantly around the fourth quarter. Since consumers account for two-thirds of all spending in the U.S., the impact on overall economic activity is large.

Real consumer wealth consists of individuals' liquid assets (including primarily cash, checking accounts, CDs, money market mutual funds, money market deposit accounts, bonds, and stocks) minus their financial liabilities (such as consumer installment debt and mortgages) plus home equity, with all three factors adjusted for inflation. Consumers have other assets also such as cars, furniture, and other items. However, these other wealth components are not considered liquid in that they cannot be easily exchanged for cash without incurring potentially large capital losses. Moreover, few people really know what these nonliquid assets could be sold for and, in practice, therefore, they tend to be more conscious of their liquid financial wealth.

The stock market is invariably the cause of most of the fluctuations in consumer wealth. The implication is that a sharp boost in stock prices today impacts consumer spending about 4-6 months later. And, since consumers account for two-thirds of the U.S. economy, the stock market's impact becomes quite pervasive. Even those consumers who do not own stock directly (which is the vast majority) are mindful of the stock market's performance through daily press reports. If the stock market is up, overall consumer confidence rises, enhancing still further money growth and inflationary pressures.

Thus, money growth and stock price movements—the two most powerful influences on the economy in the short run—feed on each other. A money increase precipitates fears of higher inflation, gradually leading to higher interest rates. The bond market acts as a natural mechanism to start bringing inflation under control by encouraging the Federal Reserve to raise short-term rates to match the already rising long-term rates. During this period interest rates can rise sharply as the Federal Reserve steps on the money brakes to stop inflation. Stock prices drop and money growth slows sharply, both leading to a recession.

The 40-60 Year Long Wave

The long-run constraints to economic growth are reflected in a 40-60 year long wave or "Kondratieff cycle," named after the early 20th century Russian economist who first discussed it. The long wave is a simple example of physics' most basic law—that, given gravity or the presence of friction, what goes up or gets started must later fall or stop. First, a money surge and the implementation of innovative new production processes set the economy off on 30-40 years of growth. But these very growth catalysts eventually checkmate the economy in later years when the Federal Reserve is forced to boost interest rates to a level that chokes inflation. The system becomes overcommitted to old, entrenched, and inefficient technology, inhibiting cost-effective and productive processes once the downward leg of the long wave takes hold. Despite the decaying capital base, high real interest rates prevent a rebuilding of the industrial complex.

It is only after a cleansing process—typically a depression in which the old technology is swept away through bankruptcies—that the Fed sheds its inflation fears and the next long cycle can begin. They then can resume pumping more money into the economy to pull us out of the depression by lowering real interest rates sharply, encouraging individuals and businesses to take the risks of spending or making long-term investments.

The long-wave cycle is ignited by resurging money growth coupled with technological innovations and/or the development of natural resources—driving forces for strong economic activity. The money surge halts the deflation process and causes very mild inflation which, at this point, is beneficial to the economy because it lowers real interest rates dramatically. For example, a 3% nominal interest rate combined with 17% deflation equates to a 20% real interest rate, stifling investment and growth. In contrast, a 3% nominal interest rate with 1% inflation equals only a 2% real interest rate, providing the catalyst for real growth.

Thus, the watershed separating depression from recovery is directly linked to when the Fed's inflationary fears subside, setting the stage for strong economic growth in the next long wave. Cheap energy and ample capital at low inflation-adjusted rates permit the creation of a massive industrial complex, providing for the efficient mass production of goods for a demanding consumer sector. And even though money growth may be relatively rapid in the early stages of a long wave, productivity is also high, preventing significant inflation from developing at this time. The money infusion stabilizes the financial arena to a point where consumer sentiment switches from saving to spending as pent-up consumer demand is brought to the fore and, thus, it stimulates more output rather than higher prices.

To meet the consumer spending surge, plant and equipment producers significantly boost their capacity by implementing the many inventions introduced late in the previous long wave. This is, in essence, supply-side economics as is commonly discussed today—but taking affect after a major depression. Concurrently, tax laws are liberalized, reflecting the Keynesian prescription for an active fiscal policy to boost the demand for greater productive capacity. As this economic demand is spurred and sufficient and efficient capacity are available, inflation is lower than it otherwise would be. In short, it is primarily during this early phase that one can experience low inflation, low interest rates, falling unemployment, and accelerating economic growth. However, this best-of-all-worlds phase for supply side and Keynesian policies only lasts during a portion of the rising years in the long wave.

The upward phase of the long wave tends to last roughly 25 years. The 50-year cycle on average then experiences a 15-year plateau with a decided downward bias as the years progress. Finally, the last 10 years or so actually evolve into a depression, completing one long-wave cycle.

Early in the downward phase of the long wave, aging equipment, institutionalized inflation through bureaucracies, political pressure to maintain rapid money growth, and higher interest rates (reflecting higher actual and expected inflation) all militate against further supply-side or Keynesian results. As the long wave matures, actual inflation and inflationary expectations intensify, monetary policy increasingly dominates the scene, and a whole series of side effects crop up. Trade protectionism rears it head, further aggravating inflationary pressures. Debt accumulation accelerates as individuals, corporations, and nations try to maintain and enhance their economic standing through greater leverage. And key markets such as stocks, housing, and energy—which in a healthier period are governed by the supplies and demands of long-term interests — become speculative avenues to beat inflation.

Very late in the Kondratieff cycle, however, the Fed

switches from an inflationary to deflationary bias. Debt servicing problems develop and speculative bubbles—such as stocks in 1929 and oil prices in 1982—burst. Individual, corporate, and international loan repudiations threaten the domestic and international banking system with collapse. Nevertheless, the Fed has no choice but to maintain high real interest rates for fear of reigniting an inflationary surge.

Initially, each liquidity crisis forces the Fed to be the "lender of last resort" by flooding the system with money to forestall a collapse. But with each successive business cycle, each money stimulus generates less and less economic growth, producing ever-shortening business expansions and lengthier recessions. In other words, the Fed must provide an ever-increasing amount of money to obtain the same rate of real economic growth. During economic contractions, the Fed can temporarily avoid an upsurge in inflationary expectations. But it doesn't take more than a very brief recovery to reignite inflationary pressures and force them right back to more restrictive monetary policies.

If the Fed doesn't act voluntarily, then, in effect, the bond market takes over and does their work for them, later forcing the Fed to raise rates anyhow. As inflationary fears accelerate, the bond market retreats, yielding the higher interest rates that the Fed is, at first, unwilling to produce. In order to defend its inflation-fighting credibility, the Fed is forced to follow the bond market's lead with a tighter monetary policy. This is symptomatic of the Fed's impotency in the face of the long wave's inherent power.

Eventually the Fed is checkmated. It is both unable and unwilling to provide the massive money injection necessary to prevent an economic collapse given its fears of precipitating a hyperinflationary surge. Meanwhile, lenders—both in the domestic and international arenas—increasingly question whether debts will be honored. Individuals, businesses and countries borrow just to service their already-burdensome debt; and anyone who gambled on ever-increasing prices finds this debt servicing prohibitively expensive once deflation sets in. The resulting liquidity crisis turns into a solvency crunch and depression. Speculative markets nosedive. And monetary authorities view themselves as powerless to supply all the money necessary to bail out the financial system.

Thus, the long wave helps explain both the current Catch-22 dilemma in which the worldwide economy is now trapped, as well as the preconditions for another period of prolonged real growth.

The 150-Year World Supremacy Cycle

Just as we saw the normal business cycle changing from decade to decade due to the hidden impact of the long wave, we find that the long wave itself is also in flux due to the influence of an even longer cycle—the 150-year world supremacy cycle. The influences of this very long cycle will have a great deal of impact on the financial, social, and political forecast for the 1990-2030 era.

It has long been known that great civilizations follow a specific and regular pattern of birth, growth, maturity, and decay; and since the late 1500s there have been only four nations—Spain, France, England, and the U.S.—that qualify for that category. In each case the world economic and political leader enjoys roughly 150 years of power. However, during periods of transition at the beginning and end of each 150-year cycle (during which three 50-year long waves typically occur), the economic and political power is not always monopolized by one nation. Rather, there tend to be overlaps where a new world leader replaces the old supreme power.

The pattern of a nation's world supremacy cycle is relatively simple. During the first of the long waves, it successfully gains unequivocal recognition as world leader. Meanwhile, the previous world power, in its third long-wave cycle, is greatly weakened by a floundering economy—old and inefficient production techniques, high inflation, little innovative genius, an overly bureaucratic state that stymies ingenuity, and an increasingly socialistic Government which is pressured to ensure a minimum standard of living for all citizens.

In contrast to this aging world leader, the newly emerging supreme nation utilizes advanced technological processes of the day to more successfully compete in world economic markets. By increasing dramatically its world market share for goods and services, the new nation gains wealth and power, thus solidifying its claim to supremacy. Typically the outgoing world power and the challenger resolve their conflict in a major war that usually develops during the third decade of the old leader's third long wave. In past centuries such wars have directly involved the vying countries. However, in recent times and probably in the future as well, the shift of power occurs without a direct conflict between the two nations. For the challenger, the confrontation occurs in its first long wave as world leader; for the aging power, it's the war that ends its reign.

Recent World Supremacy Cycles

SPAIN	1580s-1730s
FRANCE	1680s-1830s
ENGLAND	1780s-1930s
U.S.	1880s-2030s

Because the new world power is inexperienced in overseeing a large, complex, and highly diversified economy that develops in its first 50-year cycle, the depression that ends this first long wave is usually of massive proportions. However, it is also the most effective in weeding out inefficient and debt-ridden industries, freeing up financial capital for innovative enterprises, and generating new production techniques and inventions for low-cost and high-quality products. It is during the nation's second 50-year cycle that a "golden era" of political power and economic wealth develops. But it is also during this period—especially in its latter stages—that vested interests, with increasing institutionalization, seek to prevent a repetition of the ruinous depression that previously occurred. As the second long wave proceeds, social safety nets are established. Protectionist trade policies are implemented. And interventions in domestic market operations abound under Government edict. Although failing to avoid the depression, these policy changes do manage to soften the world leader's second depression—but at a cost.

This time around, the depression is not deep enough to thoroughly eradicate inefficient and debt-ridden companies because Government policies are designed to prop up the economy, rather than let it spiral downward as in its first depression as world leader. Thus, typically speaking, this "second depression" is roughly only one-third the magnitude of the "first depression" experienced about 50 years earlier. Because companies that should have failed are artificially kept from closing their doors, the sufficient financial capital needed to properly rebuild the aging industrial complex is not forthcoming. The new, innovative techniques that do get implemented are far fewer than witnessed following the first depression. Inflationary pressures—already highly imbedded—are never completely cleansed. Consequently, as the nation moves into the third long wave, high inflation results in a stagnant economy, producing a "window of vulnerability" for another country seeking economic and political supremacy.

The Outlook for the 1980s

The outlook for the next several years is guided by the increasing downward pressures of sharply slower money growth in a money-starved economy, producing frequent recessions, soaring business failures, international and domestic debt defaults, historically high real interest rates, an oil-price collapse, and disinflation followed by outright deflation. All these factors precipitate a banking collapse resulting in a U.S.

depression, lasting 5-10 years, with as much as a 20-25% unemployment rate peak before the majority of the shakeout is complete.

No one can predict the actual sequence of events. But the general scheme can be anticipated to some degree. Because we are late in the long cycle, inflation expectations are particularly sensitive to any acceleration in money growth. As soon as lay or professional investors sense the Fed will not or cannot tighten its policy due to a weak economy, the resulting expectation and later fulfillment of higher money growth leads to heightened inflation fears. Stock prices surge as greater money growth and lower interest rates boost economic activity with the help of the "buy-now-in-advance-of-higher-prices-later" syndrome. This forces the Fed to raise interest to precipitate a recession and slow inflation.

The Fed is repeatedly putting out brush fires late in the long cycle. In 1981-82 when economic activity plunged, leading to business failures, a liquidity squeeze, and a possible collapse of the financial system, the Fed allowed short-term interest rates to drop sharply, precipitating a money surge of unprecedented proportions. But the massive money infusion by the Fed needed to stabilize the economy yielded a climate conducive to an inflation acceleration. Aware of that danger, the Fed then reversed itself once again in mid-1983 to check inflation fears by invoking a tighter monetary policy through significantly slower money growth.

This then triggers an even more serious set of problems than generated by the previous monetary restraint, leading to an earlier than usual recession. However, because the Fed has, in effect, already used up its ammunition with the 1982-83 money supply explosion, it will not be able to repeat these actions to quickly end the mid-1980s recession for fear of igniting double-digit inflation later. Thus, towards the very end of a long-wave cycle, we see that monetary policy ironically becomes impotent due to its own sheer power. The money injection which would be necessary to prevent the collapse becomes so massive it is not even contemplated as a viable policy alternative for fear of aggravating inflationary pressures.

This stage will probably be experienced in the mid-1980s. Domestic and international financial participants increasingly question whether debts will be honored. The survival of countries and businesses that gambled on ever escalating prices early in the long wave is now threatened by expensive debt servicing needs. The resulting liquidity crisis turns into a solvency crunch and then into a depression as speculative markets collapse, reducing personal wealth and leading to a massive retrenchment in consumer spending.

All these processes are converging in the middle of the decade to produce a depression in the second half of the 1980s. First, the international financial system is drawing closer and closer towards a total collapse. Second, the domestic economies of each nation are being built on a house of cards as creditors keep extending unpayable debts hoping that economic conditions improve. Third, as these creditors begin to realize that any economic recovery cannot be sustained, the flow of loan money is cut off, precipitating a bust as the very foundation of the house of cards falls. International bankers and other lenders are already going this route.

Later in the process, depositors switch funds from banks, thrifts, stocks, and non-Treasury money-market funds into Treasury securities—a "flight to quality" which merely deepens the depression without resolving the fiscal woes of the Federal Government. For the time being, the liquidity crisis is being defused by emergency loans from major international institutions. At some time, however, the economic system snaps due to its inability to handle the sharp economic contractions and expansions, which are signs of an increasingly unstable economic environment.

In 1929, the stock market crash served as a catalyst for the debacle. This time, although stock prices should also decline, it is oil prices which are playing the key role. Too many world participants have bet on continually rising oil prices, just as too many speculated on continually rising stock prices in the

1920s. In 1982 we witnessed the impact of a relatively modest 7% drop in oil prices—the inability, six months later, of Mexico to repay its debts since its expenditure commitments (based on continually rising oil price expectations) far outpaced its actual cash receipts. Meanwhile, the U.S. dollar remained strong despite a widening trade deficit as these and other international uncertainties spurred a "flight to quality." Foreigners rushed to purchase dollars and invest their funds in U.S. Government securities. But this merely put further downward pressures on oil prices. A strong U.S. dollar forced these countries to use more of their currency to buy dollar-priced oil imports while, at the same time, making it even more difficult to meet their dollar-denominated debts.

It is this vicious circle, still in full swing as of late 1983, which is one of the factors making an international financial collapse inevitable. Already, many oil-related companies around the world are near bankruptcy or have actually failed as a result of the 1982 oil-price drop.

For example, Dome Petroleum of Canada is still teetering despite massive Canadian Government support. To make matters worse, Canada has been forced to institute restrictive economic policies to control double-digit inflation leading to double-digit unemployment in its place. Thus, both Canada and Mexico, the first and third largest U.S. trading partners, are being forced into severe and prolonged austerity programs, sharply reducing their demand for our exported goods. When coupled with the strong U.S. dollar, this has severely impacted our trade balance and has had a sharp negative impact on overall U.S. economic growth.

Within the U.S., the oil-price drop also caused many domestic energy producers to go bankrupt. Penn Square Bank, which was heavily loaned up to dubious oil concerns, failed. And several major U.S. money-center banks were badly burned by loans they bought from Penn Square. So as one can see, a relatively small drop in oil prices has had major worldwide repercussions.

Then, right on the heels of the first oil-price decline,

another drop developed in early 1983 with OPEC prices falling roughly 9½% from $32+ to about $29 per barrel. Despite a rapid 1983 economic rebound in the U.S., the major problems incurred by an oil-price decline still developed, although in a much more muted form than they otherwise would have. Again, right on schedule, six months after the second oil-price drop, a second wave of the international debt crisis burst onto the scene. Energy-related bank earnings slumped due to energy-loan charge-offs. Brazil was unable to service its debt ·or implement necessary austerity programs at home. In addition, nations impacted in the earlier wave, such as Mexico, saw their recessions turn into depressions. As more and more countries enter depressionary conditions, worldwide trade slumps and again negatively impacts domestic real GNP growth.

Finally, as of late 1983, we can already see the initial signs of a third round of oil-price declines. What happens if OPEC oil prices plummet from a current average of $29 per barrel to $19 per barrel as projected for the mid-1980s? This 35% drop — five times greater than the previous one—quickly leads to a depression. Prices of oil stocks plummet, dragging other issues down as well and causing a sharp drop in U.S. and worldwide consumer wealth. Within roughly 6 months, consumer spending screeches to a halt. Oil producing countries then experience a massive decline in their revenues which, in turn, forces them to slash purchases of foreign goods. Our exports plummet.

Due to budgetary problems within the U.S., the U.S. Government might invoke an oil-import tax to recoup lost revenue, preventing U.S. consumers from reaping the full benefits of lower-priced gasoline and heating oil. Then, once such protectionism starts, other nations would invoke similar trade restrictions resulting in higher inflation, lower output, and weaker export demand for all nations. It is well known that the Hawley-Smoot Act of 1930 resulted in almost a 50% increase in the effective rate of import duties between 1929-1932—a trade war often viewed as a major cause of the Great

Depression's severity. What is not commonly recognized is that trade restrictions — whether voluntarily invoked or inadvertently imposed by bodies such as the IMF—are common very late in the long-wave cycle as countries try to protect their own turf at a time of economic crisis and politically expensive unemployment.

Many assume countries would not default on their foreign debts under any circumstance because they realize they would be blacklisted from the international lending club. However, historical precedents such as Argentina's defaults in each of the past 3 depressions suggest just the opposite. Since the strong U.S. dollar forces less developed nations to use a progressively greater portion of their currency reserves to service dollar denominated debts, they are, in essence, in the same predicament as the oil producing countries.

The alternatives facing each troubled nation are to: (1) implement—even before their citizens have digested the 1982-83 measures —further drastic austerity programs, or (2) ask for 20-30 year loan extensions with near-term interest and principal payments waived, or (3) simply repudiate the country's foreign bonds and loans. The first choice would be political dynamite in countries with a history of political instability. On the other hand, there is neither convincing historical precedent nor rational cause for them to choose to repudiate their debt, although it has happened occasionally. Instead a substantial lengthening of the loan commitment is negotiated, meaning the country technically defaults on the original terms of the loan but does eventually pay it back.

What causes the third and fatal oil price decline? First, in an attempt to bolster their lagging revenues, OPEC and non-OPEC nations leapfrog one another in oil production to obtain a bigger share of a shrinking market. Second, past strength in the U.S. dollar, which has a maximum negative impact on oil demand with about a 1½ year lag (by making it more expensive in foreign nations), begins to sharply depress oil demand in the mid-1980s. Third, a sooner-than-normal U.S. recession causes overall worldwide oil demand to plunge early in this decade's second half. And even while consumption declines, revenue-hungry oil producers continue resisting production cutbacks. The only possible result is a drastic oil price drop. Therein lies one of the key reasons why a depression starting in the mid-1980s is very possible.

What many analysts fail to recognize is that even the world oil crises can be traced back to the U.S. Federal Reserve. It was approximately 2 years after the U.S. started its large 1976-1979 money infusion that OPEC oil prices soared in a lagged response to the sharp decline of the U.S. dollar which boosted worldwide demand for oil. And not coincidently, it was also about 2 years after the Fed invoked its historically restrictive monetary policy in late 1979 that OPEC oil prices began to fall — an unheard of possibility only a few years earlier. Now the stage is set for a mid-1980s oil price collapse given the sharp money slowdown in 1983's second half.

There is a second, although less likely, trigger for a depression—a dramatic change in consumer psychology vis-a-vis their homes. Actually, this scenario will probably develop concurrently with the overall depression rather than precipitate it. As is true with any slumping industry, the price of its products is also forced down. This is especially a real danger in the case of housing. What will consumers do when they see the value of their home equity decline? People who try to sell their homes will be startled to see they are netting far less than they expected or may actually incur a capital loss (which is not tax deductible)—a shocking experience which has already happened to many families during the past two recessions. In previous decades housing prices continued to rise sharply, even during recessions. But those days are gone. Now home prices do not even match the overall inflation rate during an economic recovery and actually fall during our increasingly frequent recessions.

Since families are house rich and cash poor, a dramatic cut or loss in their home equity, a major source of their savings, forces them to take drastic actions. First they cut spending to build cash savings back to what they perceive to be a comfortable level, equivalent to what they enjoyed prior to the housing market collapse. This makes the initial recession even worse. Second, homeowners attempt to minimize their losses by unloading their homes. Obviously if everybody tries to sell at the same time, home prices collapse, not unlike stocks in 1929-30. During an economic recovery, the likelihood of such a development is remote. But the probability of a consumer-led downward spiral increases dramatically during each successive recession.

For individuals, corporations, and nations the remaining years of this decade will reward those who become cash rich by retrenching, paying off debts, cutting costs, and solidifying their markets now. Conversely, it will heavily penalize those who are cash poor, heavily in debt, and committed to an overexpansion of their operations. Hence, the number one recommendation for all economic participants is to build liquid reserves to the maximum possible. In the coming deflationary environment you will want security. You will want to ensure the safety of your principal. Your first priority, therefore, will be survival—not maximum return or speculative profit.

Don't count on the Government and their various "policy options." As stated earlier, Federal officials have historically been unable to control the economy, simply because no policy can prevent the long wave from following its natural course; and, in the long run, it is a waste of time to even try. In fact, it's safe to say that any such attempts are actually counterproductive; that the best policy is to minimize the damage by speeding the depression on earlier than otherwise; and that the sooner the depression can clean out the economy, the better it is for everybody. Like a toothache, the pain is inevitable, but the decay—and the pain as well—only get worse with every delay in correcting the problem.

The 1980s will be known as the heyday of the hatchetmen — those that can successfully build cash reserves by curtailing operations to the bare bones, both in reaction to current bad times and in anticipation of still worse future conditions. Although resented for being thick-skinned and unapologetic, for laying off employees, for cutting long-standing supplier contracts, for being hard-nosed wage bargainers with remaining employees, and for hurting local economies, it is these individuals—first surfacing at the corporate level—who are the ones destined to lead us out of the economic calamity.

As corporations increasingly take this route, more and more individuals find themselves unemployed or with sharp pay cuts. Either way, the implication is that individuals are themselves forced to become hatchetmen in their own households. In the past 10-15 years, Americans have maintained their high standard of living despite rapid inflation by evolving into two-wage-earner families. But such an escape hatch can only be used once. This time, when layoffs and pay cuts hit, consumers have no choice but to sharply reduce their total spending, become renters rather than buyers of homes, and even return to the one-car family. As the effects of the plunging housing and auto industries ripple through the economy, the downward spiral forces more and more individuals to curtail spending further.

Meanwhile, local, state, and Federal Governments see their revenue bases shrink while costs resulting from the depression soar. Huge deficits result. For those state and local Governments precluded by law from having a deficit, their only possible course of action is to slash spending. But despite such efforts, state and local Governments go bankrupt due to the severe financial strains, and those who own bonds on these defunct Governmental units wind up holding worthless paper—a further sharp blow to consumer wealth and another nail in the economy's coffin. Consequently, those individuals now holding tax-exempt bonds should sell them before such defaults occur.

The key for individuals, corporations, and nations is to do the slashing or selling voluntarily now, before it is forced upon you in an unfavorable environment later. By cutting now, you can build up cash reserves to survive the depression and redirect resources into the most productive area to better take advantage of the ensuing recovery.

The first order of business is to clean house well in

advance, liquidating for cash all those assets or belongings you could live comfortably without. For those who pass this first test, there is an opportunity to take advantage of the bad times. The couple that passed up the $120,000 dreamhouse—along with the $100,000 mortgage—in 1980 and instead built up their cash, can buy that same house for 30-60% less during the depths of the depression. But the next couple in line—the one which did buy that dreamhouse—is unable to make the inflated payments when household income is cut by unemployment, pay cuts, and/or pay freezes. To avoid foreclosure—or because of it—houses like these are dumped on the market, with any price received being better than nothing. Thus, the opportunity is there to pick a bargain—provided you have the cash, while those still in debt when the depression arrives forfeit their destiny to others.

Where do you keep the liquid resources you are accumulating? The goal is to maximize safety and to preserve your principal — not to maximize yield. Your assets should be in a form that can be quickly converted to cash without risk of a major loss. Since financial markets are already too volatile to guess the best time to get in and out, this means you should forgo investments in stocks, corporate bonds, municipal bonds, commercial paper, gold, silver, other commodities, housing, or positions in the futures markets. If that means you miss a record speculative boom in the stock market or a six-month rally in the bond market, so be it. Such is the price you pay for the top safety in an era of maximum danger.

Sure, such purchases temporarily looked good in 1983. But how will they look in 1984 or 1985? Few people remember the record stock market rally of 1928-1929. Rather, history remembers the ensuing crash where the earlier winners lost everything. The profits are forgotten. Yes, key interest rates fall sharply and some bond prices soar in a depression. But will the corporation or municipality be around to repay the bond upon maturity—let alone meet interest payments during the life of the bond?

By avoiding the speculative markets, you are indeed

limiting your potential return, and compared to the performance of others around you, that realization may be hard to swallow—until, that is, the depression actually develops. Regardless of the speculative booms here and there, if you know the depression's approach is imminent and you see that the conditions for it are all there, then prudence says: "Sacrifice the high investment return for safety. Ensure your principal now so you can weather the storm later."

Virtually all savings or investment accounts at banks and thrift institutions should also be avoided. Do not be fooled by the FDIC or FSLIC insurance which supposedly insure deposits up to $100,000. That is fine for stable periods when bank failures are few. During a depression, however, many banks collapse or all are forced to close their doors temporarily. In either case, your checking account, NOW account, savings account, money-market deposit account, money-market certificates, or CDs could all be lost or inaccessible—just at the time you will need or want them the most. Since the FDIC and FSLIC insurance funds only cover about 1-2% of total deposits outstanding in the financial system, the risk of losing one's life savings is dependent on whether your bank or S&L is a survivor or loser. If a major economic collapse develops, the insurance is meaningless.

Whether you are an individual, corporation, municipality or state Government, the only places you should invest your funds are three-month Treasury bills where the Government requires a $10,000 minimum or a nonbank money market mutual fund that invests exclusively in short-term Treasury securities. Treasury bonds are only appropriate as a long-term safe investment, and should not be considered part of your liquid portfolio. This is because during the depression's early stages, banks and other financial institutions unload their Treasury notes and/or bonds to shore up their cash-flow problems. As a result, bond prices drop sharply, and if you are forced to sell at this point, you would probably incur a large capital loss. However, as a long-term investment—especially if purchased during this period of lower prices—your Treasury bond or note is virtually guaranteed of a substantial capital gain.

The 21st Century

After the U.S. depression of the 1980s, the U.S. enters the third and final long wave of its supremacy cycle. Not unlike Spain, France, and England before us, our political and economic power is already waning as our highly imbedded inflation prevents us from competing effectively in world markets. Our efforts to provide for our citizens' welfare via social security, unemployment insurance, direct welfare payments, and other social programs have drained resources and established a counterproductive bureaucracy. Later in the 21st century, as the third decade of this third long wave approaches, pressures for a direct or, more likely, indirect war with an emerging world power grow more intense.

Unless drastic and specific actions are undertaken now, the danger is great that during the first 50 years of the 21st century, America's reign as the world economic and political leader transfers to another power; and as is demonstrated in detail later, it is the Soviet Union which is the most likely candidate. But we can prevent this from taking place. To do so will require a significant amount of self-inflicted social and economic pain—necessary steps which historical precedent suggests will not be taken. However, if such steps can be conveyed to the electorate and accepted, we can use the housecleaning process of the depression to our advantage and halt Russia's expansionist tendencies.

The most straightforward way to stop Russia's rise to world supremacy is for the U.S. to engineer a 1980s depression that is sharper and longer than the 1930s debacle. By so doing, the U.S. invokes a massive housecleaning—eliminating the many debt-ridden and inefficient companies and producing a deflationary period of such magnitude that, upon coming out of the depression, hyperinflationary fears are eradicated. Because of the extensive housecleaning, abundant financial capital is available to rebuild our antiquated industrial base while, at the same time, greatly reducing our dependence upon expensive and supply-shock prone oil. Innovative new production techniques should restore our slice of the world economic pie, ensuring our wealth and political influence with which Russia could not effectively compete.

However, the likelihood of the U.S. electorate allowing a massive depression is, at this time, low. The only other alternative is for the U.S. to pick a Western industrialized nation to be our successor, to which we would provide all the necessary support and training. The selected successor nation would then vie with Russia in a battle for economic supremacy. Through subsequent analysis, Australia is shown to be the only Western candidate to come close to meeting the requirements for this role. However, as is noted later, the probability of this development is even more remote than that of a deeper 1980s depression engineered by the U.S.

Consequently, as an analyst whose tools are limited primarily to the study of actual historical precedent and the weighing of relative probabilities, one has no choice but to project that the Soviet Union will win the mantle of world supremacy from the U.S. during the next half century.

2

How the Key
Decision-Makers Are
Losing Control

Although the U.S. economy is massively detailed, its essential components can be traced to just a few active players and a simple chain of events. But rather than being an unchanging relationship, there is an everchanging or dynamic evolution that takes place among the players and the way they impact economic activity—a change which occurs in a relatively predictable fashion over the long 40-60 year period. In the short run, the players and their impacts appear to be unaltered from one business cycle to the next. But subtle differences creep in with each passing year.

Consequently, a policy change enacted today leads to far different results than the same policy decision implemented 10 or 20 years ago. Since policymakers and their economic advisers do not recognize the dynamic framework under which we live, it is not too surprising that the Government is unable to redirect the economy into a perpetual state of rapid economic growth, low inflation, low interest rates, and full employment. Rather, the mere fact that such a golden era is assumed to be possible at all times implies a collection of players with an unchanging interaction among themselves and an inflexible posture towards the economy. History and current economic events prove just the opposite.

Herein lies the key stumbling block of the monetarist, Keynesian, and supply-side economic theories that permeate our educational and policymaking institutions today. All implicitly assume a static rather than dynamic world. But before one can analyze the economy in its everchanging mode, the "stop action" explanation of the economic flows over a very short period must be understood.

The key players in the U.S. economy—as well as any economic system of an industrialized Western nation—include the Federal Reserve, the bond market, the stock market, the foreign exchange market, and the consumer. These institutions, markets, or groups represent the interactions provided by money growth, human psychology, speculation, economic growth, and inflation, as depicted in more detail below. They are discussed in static terms initially to explain the general framework under which the economy operates. Later, they are reviewed in a dynamic framework which takes into account changes or variations that occur as the long wave progresses.

The Federal Reserve

When all is said and done, the most powerful influence on the economy comes from the Federal Reserve—not the President, Congress, or political pressures in general. It is the Federal Reserve that regulates the all-important amount of money that flows into the economy.

Within the Federal Reserve, two interrelated decision-making bodies comprise the center of power. The seven members of the first group, the Board of Governors, are appointed by the President and confirmed by the Senate for 14-year terms, and thus enjoy a long length of service designed to remove Federal Reserve decisions from short-run political pressures. The chairperson of the seven Board members serves a renewable 4-year term (which is not currently coincident with the Presidential election cycle) and invariably imprints his philosophy on the Board to such a degree that it is rare for his views to be overruled by his colleagues.

The second decision-making group, the Federal Open Market Committee or FOMC, consists of the seven Board of Governors plus five Presidents of the twelve Federal Reserve banks that comprise the Federal Reserve System. Of these five, four rotate every year so that over a three-year period each one has an opportunity to be a voting member. In addition, the President of the New York Federal Reserve Bank is a permanent member of this group for various technical reasons.

The FOMC meets approximately ten times per year to review economic conditions and vote upon the appropriate amount of money to be supplied to the economy. Since 1976, the group must announce money growth targets for the year by law. In reality the Fed sets several targets for various measures of money, with various gradations from the most liquid (such as cash) to relatively less liquid mediums (such as bank CDs). The most important money measure is M-1, consisting primarily of consumers' and businesses' holdings of cash, demand deposits, NOW, and Super-NOW accounts.

The Real Causes of Inflation and Recession

Money growth impacts real economic activity with a 4-6 month lag and inflation with a 1½ year delay. This dual impact is the source of the eternal policy conflict faced by the Fed. The positive impact of money pumped into the economy to lower interest rates, boost economic activity, and reduce the unemployment rate over the near term, is later reversed when that money is converted into price inflation which then leads to higher interest rates, lower economic growth, and higher unemployment. The following graphs show money growth's relationship to the economy and inflation.

The first chart shows how money's 6-month growth rate (annualized) closely correlates with total industrial production

6 months later; how money growth is a key leading indicator of subsequent production and overall economic trends.

The two inflation graphs show that year-over-year money growth (with and without oil price movements) impacts the year-over-year inflation rate 1½ years later. In subsequent chapters it is demonstrated that Fed decisions determine OPEC oil price movements—thus, the reason for incorporating oil prices with M-1 in determining inflation. However, for argument's sake now, the close relationship between money growth alone and inflation is also depicted. In either case, money growth is obviously the major determinant of inflation about 18 months hence.

Most economists and policymakers utilize the traditional cost-plus approach to explain inflation, attributing relatively little importance to money. The traditional view is that inflation filters throughout the economy as wages rise and prices of a product's inputs increase. At each stage, a cost-plus increase is invoked, eventually leading to higher inflation at the consumer level.

Economists traditionally explain these pressures in reference to the nation's capacity to produce. In their view, if a business is underutilizing its capital and labor, prices do not rise; whereas if a business is running near full capacity, price hikes are common. Therefore, traditional economists prefer controlling inflation with fiscal policy solutions and possibly wage/price restraints.

But the cost-plus analysis inaccurately identifies the true source of inflation—excessive money growth to spur economic activity and to reduce the unemployment rate—a simple case of too much money chasing too few goods. As money growth accelerates, economic demand also rises after a 4-6 month delay. The resulting increased sales reduce the inventory stocks of retailers which, if confirmed by still further increases in demand, motivate them to rebuild their inventories by placing new orders with wholesalers and manufacturers. Wholesalers and manufacturers, in turn, now incur higher than normal sales resulting in a rundown of their inventories. It is a ripple

CHART 2.1. MONEY GROWTH PREDICTS INDUSTRIAL PRODUCTION

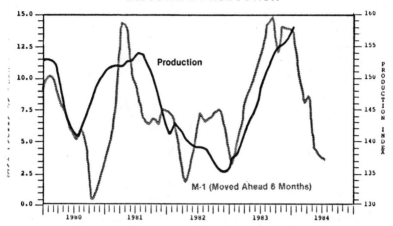

Money supply growth (i.e. M-1) is the most potent force impacting the U.S. economy in the short run, affecting economic activity with a 4 to 6 month delay. Therefore, in this graph, the M-1 growth rate is pushed ahead 6 months to show its close relationship to subsequent production trends. Data Source: Federal Reserve.

CHART 2.2. MONEY GROWTH PREDICTS CONSUMER PRICE INFLATION (YEAR-OVER-YEAR GROWTH RATES)

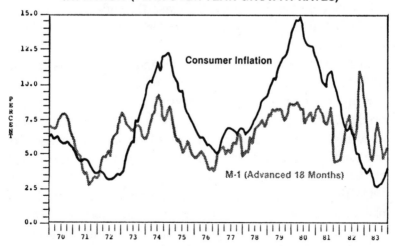

Although M-1 growth has a sharp impact on real economic activity in the short run, its most significant long-run effect is on inflation which, as you can see here, is translated into consumer price increases about 1½ years later. Thus, it is clear that inflation is largely a monetary phenomenon. All data in the chart represent year-over-year growth rates. Data Source: Federal Reserve, Commerce Dept.

**CHART 2.3. MONEY AND OIL PRICE GROWTH COMBINED
AS PREDICTORS OF CONSUMER PRICE INFLATION**

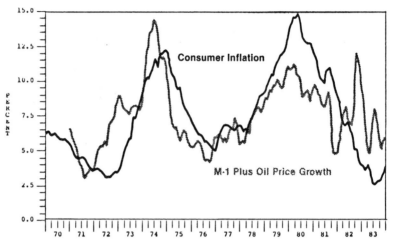

Within the econometric model used to generate this book's forecast, consumer price inflation is projected using the combination of year-over-year growth rates for (a) M-1 of 18 months earlier plus (b) oil price movements. Oil price trends themselves are traced back to U.S. monetary policy actions through past changes in the U.S. dollar and overall U.S. economic demand. Data Source: Federal Reserve, Commerce Dept.

effect of the overall demand increase through the various levels of production which finally comes to the primary stage—raw materials.

In the raw materials market, demand also exceeds the supplies on hand, boosting prices. For manufacturers, the higher raw material prices then increase the cost to produce their product, forcing them to raise the price to the wholesaler who, in turn, must raise the price to retailers; and so on down the line to the consumer who must spend more for the desired product.

On the surface, it appears that the traditional cost-plus explanation for inflation is correct—the raw material price increase seems responsible for the eventual consumer price rise. However, at each production or sales stage, it is the higher economic demand that precipitates the need to rebuild inventories; and this higher economic demand is originally spurred by the additional money pumped into the economy. Rather than the cost-plus cycle being responsible for the increase in inflation, it is actually the initial money boost which increases demand and starts the whole chain of events described above.

Many analysts raise the question: "How can M-1 or money supply growth be the principle cause of inflation when we have OPEC and its sharp influence on domestic inflation through oil prices?" What they generally do not recognize is that oil price movements are themselves a direct result (with a lag) of U.S. monetary policy. Chart 2.4 shows the relationship between the U.S. dollar (inverted) and oil price movements about 1½ years later.

In the 1970s, excessive money growth drove up the U.S. economy and boosted worldwide economic demand with a 6-12 month lag. This, in and of itself, would have been enough to force oil prices up. However, the additional consequence of the excessive money growth—the sharp drop in the U.S. dollar—further encouraged an oil price increase. Since OPEC oil is priced and paid for in U.S. dollars, and since nations could buy more U.S. dollars with each unit of their currency, oil bought by foreign nations became relatively cheap, further boosting oil demand and increasing the pressures for more price hikes. Therefore, it is no mere coincidence that the oil price surges of 1974 and 1979-80 were preceded by surging U.S. money growth and a plunging U.S. dollar.

Conversely, in the 1980s, the tight monetary policy invoked in recent years has resulted in a record high U.S. dollar and, again, about 1½ years later, a sharp oil-price drop, with the process described above working in reverse. In fact, despite oil price cuts in dollar terms, most importing nations have still had to pay more in terms of their own currencies, further depressing demand.

As indicated earlier, the U.S. dollar is affected by monetary policy through interest rates. The next chart demonstrates this relationship. The real, or inflation-adjusted, Fed funds rate, which reflects both current and past monetary policy, explains movements in the U.S. dollar. The degree of tightness or ease in monetary policy is first apparent in nominal interest rates, and then, after 1½ years in inflation as well, thereby impacting real interest rates.

Now, by combining the conclusions from charts 2.4 and 2.5, oil price movements can be easily traced back to their original source—U.S. monetary policy of 18 months ago. (In the past year the relationship between oil prices and the U.S. dollar has not been as close because OPEC has chosen to cut production more than prices. But even under this situation, monetary policy is still greatly impacting OPEC decision making, whether it be through pricing or production.)

How the Federal Reserve's monetary policy influences the economy leads us to the remaining links in the chain. As discussed earlier, the Fed regulates money growth in an attempt to direct economic activity on a noninflationary path. The next several paragraphs describe in greater detail the actual steps the Fed undertakes to accomplish this task. Two scenarios will be reviewed—one where economic activity and inflation are overheating, and another where a recession with sharply slowing inflation or outright deflation is in progress.

When the economy and inflation are rapidly accelerating, the Fed wants to slow both processes to prevent hyperinflation. The general procedure is for the Fed to supply less money to the economy than they were previously providing. Without the money to spend, the economy slows significantly (with a lag), after which inflationary pressures also ease. However, inflation has never been fundamentally and successfully slowed except by a recession or depression.

First, to reduce inflation, the Fed lowers its money growth target range to a level which leads to slower economic activity. Second, the Fed undertakes technical steps designed to reduce actual money growth to the desired range. Third, the reduction in money available to the economy pushes up the Fed funds rate and forces banks to cut back on their lending. Fourth, the higher Fed funds rate causes an upward adjustment of all interest rates from short-term Treasury bill rates to long-term Treasury bond rates, from commercial paper rates to corporate bond yields, from CD rates to the prime

CHART 2.4. THE U.S. DOLLAR PREDICTS OIL PRICES

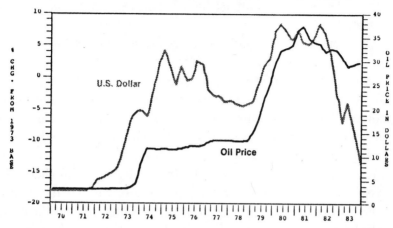

Movements in the U.S. dollar (inverted and advanced six quarters in the chart) impact oil pricing and production decisions with about a 1½ year lag. In 1983-84, this relationship has not been as close because OPEC has cut production rather than cutting prices. However, the key is that monetary policy is still impacting OPEC decision making, whether it be through pricing or production. Data Source: Morgan Guaranty Bank, Commerce Dept.

CHART 2.5. THE REAL FED FUNDS RATE
PREDICTS THE U.S. DOLLAR

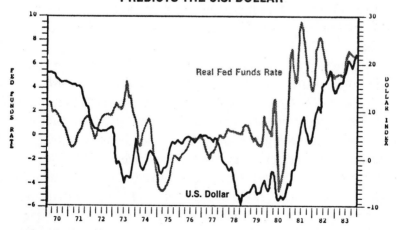

The U.S. dollar is affected by monetary policy through inflation-adjusted interest rates. However, this must be viewed in conjunction with the trade surplus/deficit and international debt problems which can also exert a large impact at times. Data Source: Federal Reserve, Morgan Guaranty Bank.

rate and to mortgage rates. Next, banks—with less money available to them—readjust their balance sheets towards fewer loans.

Higher interest rates depress bond prices which, by definition, move inversely to interest rates. Stock prices fall because higher interest rates imply slower economic activity in the future, depressing corporate profits and resulting in lower dividend payouts. The U.S. dollar, however, rallies on news of higher interest rates since dollar-denominated investments now yield a higher return relative to foreign currencies, attracting foreign investors who bid up its price. In short, the Fed's lowering of its target range in order to limit future money growth has widespread repercussions in the financial markets.

The higher price of credit, the curtailment of its availability, and the resulting decline in consumer wealth (due to lower stock and bond prices) reduce real economic activity and, later, lead to slower inflation. As shown in succeeding graphs, the stock market is the key variable behind the fluctuations in wealth which, in turn, correlates very closely with economic activity about two quarters later. Putting the two together, the stock market's impact on consumer spending— representing two-thirds of the U.S. economy—is obviously quite important.

In reaction to the consumer spending decline, businesses begin to liquidate inventories and cut back on any new orders for goods. Thus, six to twelve months after the initial Fed money draining action designed to slow inflation, the bulk of the economy—including consumer spending, housing activity, and business expenditures—is in a solid retracement.

At this point, interest rates are impacted by a secondary but often more important aftereffect of the initial policy decision—weaker credit demands and negative economic activity causing money growth to fall below the Fed's target range. The Fed lowers interest rates by adding more money to the economy, which sets the stage for halting the economic decline. Finally, after a 1½ year lag, the maximum effect of

CHART 2.6. STOCK MARKET PREDICTS CONSUMER WEALTH

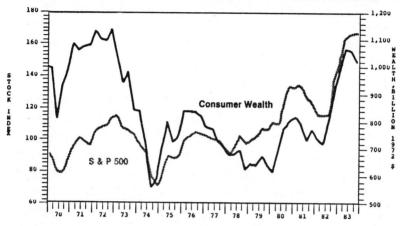

Changes in stock prices are the main determinant of movements in real consumer financial wealth. Even though stock market movements initially represent paper profits or losses, the impact on wealth is quite significant and is quickly translated into consumer spending and overall economic activity. Data Source: Standard and Poor, Commerce Dept.

CHART 2.7. REAL CONSUMER WEALTH PREDICTS REAL GNP

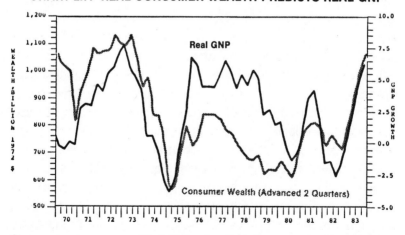

Changes in consumer wealth (which primarily reflect movements in the stock market) have a very strong impact on consumer spending about 4-6 months hence. Since consumer spending accounts for two thirds of real GNP, real consumer financial wealth correlates very closely with year-over-year real GNP growth two quarters later. Data Source: Federal Reserve, Commerce Dept.

the initial money slowdown also acts to reduce inflation. The inflation slowdown plus all the previous economic and market impacts now come back full circle to once again influence the Fed's decisions concerning the appropriate money growth target.

An entirely different sequence of events evolves under recessionary conditions. In this case, the Fed raises the money growth target to permit a decline in interest rates which boosts expenditures on consumer durables, housing, inventories, and plant and equipment. However, following the initial 1-6 month interest rate decline, the secondary (and again more important) impact of the money policy change tends to push interest rates back up again, as accelerating money growth and higher economic demand spur inflationary fears and, later, the Fed's own countermeasures. Particularly in the 1980s— corresponding to a very late stage of the long wave—Fed countermeasures have been strong enough to completely reverse the economic gains sparked by the initial money increase.

Summary: How the Economy Operates

Money growth, interest rates, and consumer wealth all act as message carriers to the economy. As a rough rule of thumb, greater money growth today leads to greater economic activity 4-6 months hence. But more importantly, rapid money growth today leads to rapid inflation roughly 1½ years later which, along with inflation expectations, tend to move interest rates. Sharp money growth tends to boost inflation expectations which, in turn, causes consumers and businesses to spend in anticipation of higher actual inflation. Obviously buying now in anticipation of inflation borrows from future expenditures. However, it is a phenomenon that can be sustained for a surprisingly long time.

The Fed tries to control inflation and the economy by steering money growth along a desired path. The logic is that money (consisting of cash and checkable deposits) represents those funds readily available to buy goods and services. If readily spendable funds are reduced, then inflationary pressures should subside sometime after the reduced money growth lowers economic activity. Over time the interest rate structure is altered due to the Fed's move. Manipulation of the Fed's money growth targets alters actual money growth which, in turn, impacts interest rates, economic demand, and prices. Interest rates represent a credit cost for housing, plant and equipment spending, and consumer durable expenditures. In addition, interest rate movements impact bond and stock price returns which directly affect consumer wealth and spending. Thus, money growth expectations are a major factor determining inflation expectations. And lastly, past actual money growth and price expectations determine future actual inflation.

The past few years are a prime illustration of both the power and negative repercussions of monetary policy and money growth. Yet some economists cling to the belief that the Fed can halt excessive money growth without severe ramifications for the unemployment rate and overall economic activity; that changes in money cause only gradual long-run changes rather than short-run movements in the business cycle. The recessions of 1980 and 1981-82—both induced by monetary policy—along with the concomitant jumps in the unemployment rate are evidence that this belief is wrong. In reality, monetary policy does have a sharp impact on short-run economic factors.

In addition to money growth, consumer wealth movements have a profound effect on the economy in the short run. Depending on how wisely past personal income receipts are invested or spent, one's stock of wealth can rise or fall. If it rises, the capital gain can be used to buy additional goods and/or investments, with the reverse occurring if a loss develops.

Over the longer run, the home equity component of wealth can have a major impact. Since consumers are, in general, house rich but cash poor, a steady decline in real home prices could have a devastating long-term impact on consumer spending and the overall economy. In this respect, a dramatic change in expectations about future housing capital gains during a depression would have a far greater impact on total wealth than the short-run impact of stock prices.

The next section discusses how the preceding pages differ from traditional explanations of the economy's operation in the short run.

The Fed's Catch-22 Dilemma

So far, monetary theory has been described in basic terms— as the strong arm of Governmental policy options, as the primary arbiter between growth vs. recessions, or rampant inflation vs. mild inflation. But this is not always the case. Contrary to traditional monetarist views, monetary theory does not continually operate in such a clean and well defined form throughout the long wave's 40-60 year expanse. There are times when monetary policy becomes impotent, unable to stem the tide of depression. Nevertheless, monetary policy is always more powerful than fiscal policy—the cornerstone of Keynesian and supply-side economic theories.

The Keynesian viewpoint is that depressions are not self-correcting, implying an inherent instability in the economy which, according to Keynes, should be overcome by the countercyclical use of Federal budget surpluses and deficits. During recessions or depressions, deficits would promote economic growth and pull us out of the slump. During periods of rapid economic activity and inflation, surpluses would counter the overheating process. Money is given little or no significance.

Time and time again, however, it has been demonstrated that monetary policy is the real force behind Government policy as Fed actions can neutralize a fiscal policy initiative, whereas the reverse does not occur. For example, if the

Administration enacts a 10% tax cut, money growth is initially boosted as individuals hold the excess funds in checking accounts in anticipation of increased spending. As long as the Fed maintains a restrictive monetary policy, the tax cut cannot provide a sustained stimulus. This is simply because the Fed must, by definition, force money growth back to its target to prevent a future inflation acceleration, letting interest rates rise to whatever level is necessary to neutralize the tax cut's stimulus. The only time it can pass through to the economy is when the Fed lets it—by permitting the extra money growth that is initially generated and acquiescing to the inflationary costs which will surface 1½ half years later. In essence, fiscal policy is a slave to monetary policy.

The 1964 tax cut was considered by many the pinnacle of Keynesian fiscal policy initiatives, given its strong positive results in boosting economic activity. However, if one looks at the economic environment prior to, and after, the 1964 tax cut, it becomes apparent that monetary policy was the real force behind the economic surge. As the summary table below indicates, money growth, real GNP, inflation, and interest rates rose. Monetary policy was very expansionary, permitting an environment conducive to the tax cut. However, the ultimate consequences were a tripling in the inflation rate and a near doubling of the nominal interest rate level as an expansionary monetary policy validated the fiscal policy action.

1964 Tax Cut: The Three Years Before And After

	Real GNP	Money Supply	CPI	3-Mo T-Bill
Period Prior to 1964 Tax Cut	+3.6%	+2.0%	+1.2%	2.82%
Period Following 1964 Tax Cut	+5.0%	+4.3%	+3.7%	4.18%

A more recent theoretical solution to the economy's woes is presented by "supply-side" economists. Supply-siders recommend tax cuts to boost investment in combination with a gold-backed U.S. dollar. In their view, this ensures desired economic growth. But it is just a repeat of the scenario when monetary authorities do not support the fiscal policy moves. Tax cuts represent an expansionary fiscal policy—but one which would be immediately countered by the extremely disciplined and highly restrictive monetary policy implied by the gold standard (assuming its rules are faithfully followed).

The Reagan Administration's 1981 policy initiatives were a slight variation from the supply-siders' theoretical prescription. The Administration believed a combination of large tax cuts, budget cuts, a rapid defense buildup, and a very strict Fed monetary policy would lead to a quick drop in inflation and inflation expectations, resulting in sharp interest rate declines, rapid economic growth, and a dramatically improved budget deficit outlook. The tight Fed policy, however, proved to be inconsistent with efforts to boost the economy.

Thus, history has proven the supply siders to be incorrect. Interest rates did not fall in early and mid-1981 as they expected. Actually, they surged because of the restrictive monetary policy to control above-target money growth and to allay the bond market's inflation fears due to expected huge Federal deficits. Nor did the economy move in the desired direction. The record high interest rates in 1981 then precipitated the 1981-82 recession, resulting in still larger budget deficits.

Where did the supply siders go wrong? Their errant forecasts can be traced to their failure to recognize that (1) monetary policy—not fiscal policy—is what determines future economic growth, interest rates, and inflation, and (2) that sharply lower interest rates, as they wanted the Federal Reserve to engineer, lead to above-target money growth and accelerating inflation.

When the Fed finally and belatedly did comply with lower interest rates in 1982 (to pull us out of the worsening recession and to avert the very threatening international debt crisis), it soon brought on above-target money growth, forcing higher interest rates again and an expected premature end to the recovery.

Looking at economic history, one observes that during certain periods a particular economic theory was adopted and seemed to work. Monetarist, Keynesian, and supply-side theories have each had their moments of glory. But their universal applicability is always fleeting. The theories themselves are not necessarily flawed. What is flawed is the idea that only one of these popular theories operates at all times. In reality, each theory has its time and place during the 40-60 year cycle. But no one viewpoint can be implemented throughout the full long wave with desired results. The economic fiascos of our times may prompt some to scrap all economic research conducted to date. However, all that is needed is a synthesis of the apparently contradictory arguments into one unified theory that does accurately operate over a long time horizon. The long wave process offers the framework for such a task.

3

The Long Wave

This chapter explains how the long wave operates and why the Fed—with all its ability to direct the economy in the short run—is unable to prevent a depression, let alone bring about a perpetual golden era. This inability to alter the long wave is due to the inherent policy clash among conflicting goals for money growth, inflation, debt servicing, and economic activity. More money growth to boost economic activity and lower unemployment leads to rampaging inflation; less money growth precipitates debt servicing problems, corporate failures, rising unemployment, and frequent recessions. Ultimately, the Fed's only choice is to prevent inflation which then causes the depression late in the long wave. Throughout the depression, the Fed is incapable of implementing strong countermeasures for fear of inducing hyperinflation but later, when the fears are finally dissipated, the depression ends as the Fed implements a money infusion program.

Thus the essence of the Kondratieff cycle is that the seed of its beginning (money growth) is eventually checkmated by its own end products (inflation and debt servicing problems). As actual inflation and inflationary expectations intensify over the

Kondratieff cycle, a whole series of secondary effects come to the fore. Wars occur with an uncanny periodicity boosting economic demand for domestic as well as war needs. Because productivity is very high due to the new, innovative, and efficient productive capacity present, inflation is lower than it otherwise would be. However, as time progresses, plant and machinery age and become inefficient relative to foreign production processes. A wave of protectionism sets in which further aggravates the inflationary pressures. Debt accumulation accelerates as individuals, corporations, and nations try to maintain and enhance their economic standing relative to others through greater leverage. Speculative markets such as stocks, housing, and oil become the avenues to beat inflation.

When Federal policy switches from an inflationary to a deflationary bias, debt servicing problems surface and speculative markets burst. Finally, individual, corporate, and international loan defaults threaten the domestic and international banking system with collapse. All the initial and secondary effects of the Kondratieff cycle interact to restrict monetary policy options, setting the stage for an unavoidable depression.

But even as the depression unfolds, other factors are already germinating to produce the next long-wave upturn. A surge in innovations and low real interest rates help establish a new, efficient production function which sustains rapid economic growth for the 30-40 years following the depression. Typically, new innovations are bunched in the depression period. But weak economic demand and a shortage of working capital prevent a rapid infusion of these new products into the economic mainstream. It is only during the first 30 years of the next long cycle that the innovations are implemented operationally, drastically changing the underpinnings of the economy and leading to accelerating growth.

Table 3.1 summarizes the timing of major events during a typical Kondratieff cycle. Each decade listed below is based on its position relative to the last depression, with the "First Decade" corresponding to the first decade following a depression. This decade dating scheme conforms well with the "very long recessions" (actually, depressions) as dated by the National Bureau of Economic Research. The table should be viewed with caution as historical data are fragmentary and at times suspect. Rather, the trends in the various series are more important than actual numerical results.

The synthesis of the monetarist, supply side, and Keynesian theories is that each theory has its own time and place during portions of the Kondratieff cycle; that no one theory can be successfully applied throughout its entirety. Supply-side economics and Keynesian policies thrive in the long cycle's upward leg (with the consent of monetary policy); monetary policy virtually takes over during the downward leg; and, finally, very late in the cycle, even the Fed's power ceases, at which time Keynesian theory's expectation of a collapse in plant and equipment investment (as their major explanation for the 1930s depression) predominates.

Thus, the various economic theories have shifting impacts as the long wave proceeds. In the early stages of the long wave, money growth is rapid but, due to high productivity, it goes into output rather than into higher prices. Earlier, high real interest rates during the depression discouraged risk-taking and spending. But now, rapid money growth stabilizes the financial arena to a point where consumer sentiment switches from saving to spending; and pent-up consumer demand is brought to the fore by sharply declining real interest rates.

To meet the consumer spending surge, plant and equipment producers significantly boost their capacity by using the innovations introduced late in the previous long wave. New and highly efficient production capacity soon follows. This is, in essence, supply-side economics as is commonly discussed today. Concurrently, tax laws are liberalized to bolster demand (an application of Keynesian views), reinforcing the more rapid money infusion. In sum, early in a long wave, one can experience low inflation, low interest rates, falling unemployment, and accelerating economic growth.

TABLE 3.1

Summary Of Long Wave Characteristics

Decade Since Depression	M-2 Money Growth (%)	Detrended Real GNP Growth (%)	Wholesale Prices (%)
1st	+ 8.0	+ 1.6	+ 1.6
2nd	+ 6.2	+ 0.7	+ 1.8
3rd	+ 7.3	+ 1.0	+ 4.0
4th	+ 6.5	- 0.1	- 1.2
5th	+ 3.0	- 3.0	- 1.9

Decade Since Depression	Wars	Political Scandals	Change in Commercial Paper Rate (basis points)
1st	None	None	- 42
2nd	Minor War	None	+ 62
3rd	Major War	None	+ 120
4th	None	Numerous	+ 111
5th	None	None	- 251

Decade Since Depression	Yield Curve (Long-Short Interest Rates) (basis points)	Real Long-Term Interest Rate (%)	Business Failure Rate (%)
1st	+ 25	1.26	0.66
2nd	- 25	1.48	0.71
3rd	- 29	0.44	0.71
4th	+ 53	7.57	0.67
5th	+ 79	6.02	0.98

NOTE: "5th Decade" equals the next depression. U.S. data are used for this and subsequent tables in the chapter.

However these positive supply-side and Keynesian phases only last during the first 20 years or so. Later in the long wave, aging equipment, institutionalized inflation through bureaucracies, political pressure to maintain rapid money growth, and higher interest rates to rein in inflationary pressures prevent a repeat of earlier supply-side and Keynesian results. As the long wave matures, monetary policy increasingly dominates movements in economic activity, inflation, and inflation expectations. Moreover, the repetition of a policy action—whether monetary or Keynesian—first attempted several business cycles earlier does not yield similar results.

The First Decade - Recovery

Each decade following the depression has specific characteristics. The first decade is marked by a conservative mood as people are unsure economic demand is sustainable following the depression experience.[2] The memories of the depression are still very strong, leading the populace to avoid risk-taking. Speculation in general is very modest as reflected in the average yearly stock market gain versus results in later decades. Presidents during these periods are generally strong and well liked. Protectionist movements, although still pervasive, are not as powerful as during the depression years.

The key is real interest rates. During the depression, when deflation was prevalent, even low nominal interest rates were effectively very high when adjusted for price trends. Now, early in the new long wave, rapid money growth is needed to actually boost inflation towards the level of nominal interest rates in order to push inflation-adjusted interest rates down sharply. It is at this stage that consumers' pent-up demand for housing and other goods and services is unleashed, bringing on the gains in real output and incomes.

Housing activity tends to jump sharply during this phase—spurred not only by the lower interest rates but also be falling unemployment, very slow price increases, larger output and incomes and, of course, rising consumer confidence. During depressions, relatives—as well as unrelated families—live together to cut costs. But once the depression is over, housing quickly emerges as one of the first priorities as families seek a home of their own. Because housing has such a dramatic ripple effect, demand for carpet, appliances, draperies, furniture, and other goods also increases. And businesses increasingly implement new innovative techniques to expand their production capacity to meet the rising consumer demand.

The Second Decade—Wealth Accumulation and War

By the time the second decade arrives, the probability of a war is greatly increased. In the previous two decades, a very conservative philosophy focuses on domestic issues and domestic spending programs to the detriment of defense planning; and, in this sense, the nation tends to be introverted and highly protectionistic. These conditions usually set the stage for war due to the general breakdown of worldwide communication and the absence of economic links. Thus, world issues, which were of secondary importance while the world economy was mired in depression, now begin to resurface in the first decade as the money surge boosts economic activity. Then, in the second decade, wars occur with a remarkable periodicity and with an uncanny similarity in magnitude, as shown in Table 3.3.

The camaraderie of a nation's people early in a long wave generally leads to strong nationalistic tendencies, strong support by the electorate, a relatively free hand by the military to conduct an all-out effort and, ultimately, a quick end to the war itself. In contrast, the wars of the third decade tend to be more protracted and more costly with large Federal budget deficits the ultimate result. Usually occurring around the time of the cycle's economic peak in growth rate terms, the wars of the third decade are largely not supported, with peace movements common, and with large segments of the population rejecting a conflict which threatens their "good life" and appears to be unjustified in the eyes of many.

The only war not to follow the long-wave pattern was

TABLE 3.2

Stock Market And Housing Starts

Decade Since Depression	Detrended Stock Market (%)	Detrended Housing Starts (%)
1st	− 2.4	+ 5.0
2nd	+ 3.4	+ 1.4
3rd	+ 1.7	− 0.5
4th	− 0.3	+ 3.4
5th	− 3.1	− 9.4

WWII which took place in the first decade after the depression; and yet it is an exception which helps prove the rule. It was the far-reaching power of monetary policy run amok which was a key factor. There are only two options for monetary policy during a long wave's downward leg: (1) Fight the economic decline by continually pumping more money into the economy leading to hyperinflation (which destroys the Government and the middle class but degenerates into depression anyway), or (2) restrict money growth to prevent an inflation acceleration even as the nation slides into a depression. Historically, there have been—and continue to be—far more cases of the deflationary choice than the hyperinflation options (which typically would not occur until the very last long wave in a country's supremacy cycle). But in the early 1920s, German political authorities resisted the long wave's path. The result was a classic hyperinflation during 1922-1923 and total chaos in Germany's political and economic systems, permitting Adolf Hitler's rise to power and leading to the unusual timing of WWII.

Similarly (but with important differences), France's hyperinflation of the 1790s led to the overthrow of the French Government and opened the way for Napoleon and his radical, power-hungry Government. This too had its rude consequences—the French-British War and the French

TABLE 3.3

Timing of Wars During First Kondratieff Cycles

Decade Since Depression	Wars
1st Decade	
1786-1795	
1836-1845	
1886-1895	
1940-1949	World War II (1941-1945)
2nd Decade	
1796-1805	War with France (1798-1799)
1846-1855	War with Mexico (1847-1848)
1896-1905	Spanish-American War (1898-1899)
1950-1959	Korean War (1951-1953)
3rd Decade	
1806-1815	War of 1812 (1812-1815)
1856-1865	Civil War (1860-1865)
1906-1919	World War I (1917-1919)
1960-1969	Vietnam War (1964-1972)
4th Decade	
1816-1825	
1866-1875	None
1920-1929	
1970-1979	
5th Decade	
1826-1835	
1876-1885	None
1930-1939	
1980-1989	

Revolution of 1848, which spilled over into other societies as well. These conflicts, however, conformed to their normal timing during long waves.

Why did the German hyperinflation, in contrast to the French inflationary bout, produce an unexpected war—one which occurred prior to the normal timing of early in the second decade or late in the third decade? One key reason is that it is atypical for hyperinflations to develop in a nation trying to become the supreme economic and political power as Germany was attempting in the 1920s. In France's case, her hyperinflation developed while she was late in her supremacy cycle.[3] The implication is that hyperinflation developing in a challenger nation, when coupled with the aggressiveness of other potential challenging nations, leads to an unexpected war as the hyperinflating nation adopts a radical and power-hungry political system.

Thus, despite a convergence of other key factors, the actual timing of WWII can be attributed to the aftereffects of the German hyperinflation with the rise of a radical new power structure that had virtually nothing to lose. Because WWII occurred when it did, the first decade's normally very slow inflation rise did not occur. Instead, rapid inflation developed as the war sharply and prematurely increased economic demand. Although the depression officially ended in March 1933, the period from 1934 to 1939 was turbulent—so much so that the lay person would probably consider it part of the depression. Thus, WWII cut short the 1934-1939 housecleaning period from spilling over into the 1940s.

It is also possible that WWII's interference may cause the current long wave to end a decade later than past ones; as shown in Table 3.4, price movements in our recent fourth decade more closely correlate to trends in the typical third decade. However, other events suggest the current long wave is on course for a 1980s depression.

Because a second decade war is relatively minor, sharp inflationary pressures do not develop, although prices do indeed begin to rise at a somewhat faster rate. Money growth, although still rapid, is slowed as monetary policy tends to lean somewhat against the wind to prevent an even sharper price acceleration at this stage. These two factors, coupled with a greater rate of economic growth, then begin to cause an interest rate rise—albeit a very modest one in contrast to the sharp increases later in the cycle. Meanwhile, the unemployment rate continues to decline and housing activity slows as the earlier pent-up demand is largely satisfied.

The nation's overriding concern during this period is towards wealth accumulation [4]; and one way to accomplish this goal is to embrace free trade or open up new markets. As past innovations become operational through new productive processes, demand from the new markets is met at lower costs leading to higher profits. Thus, the initial money infusion has set the stage for strong corporate profits which, in turn, result in second decade stock price increases which tend to be the most rapid of the entire cycle. (A brief, speculative surge late in the fourth decade, just prior to the depression, can yield large gains but, due to its short and transitory nature, it does not boost significantly the decade-long averages.)

The Third Decade - Prosperity and War

The third decade contains the most rapid rate of real economic growth during the Kondratieff cycle; but it is this period's prosperity which contributes to significant domestic and international unrest. The industrial base developed early in the long wave—to meet (1) pent-up consumer demand and (2) the needs of a war economy early in the second decade—begins to depreciate as time passes. At the same time, the nation, comfortable with the wealth buildup achieved thus far, turns its attention to social reform and other progressive issues.[5] In other words, the political mood is to prosper from the past decade's wealth accumulation. To do this and to prevent an economic slowdown, however, the monetary authorities are forced to boost the rate of money growth which, unlike earlier in the long wave, begins to have a greater impact on inflation than on real economic activity.

Average real economic growth is somewhat greater in the

third decade than in the second, but this small extra boost comes at a large cost as inflation accelerates dramatically and the nation's available resources are taxed with expensive social programs.

Finally, late in the third decade, this liberal mood culminates in "guns-and-butter" programs as a major war develops. Inflationary problems intensify as domestic and war demands are met with a plant and equipment buildup which relies upon outdated and inefficient production techniques along with rapid money growth to support the war effort. Interest rates rise fairly sharply due to higher inflationary expectations, although real interest rate levels are still relatively low. The unemployment rate reaches its bottom; while housing activity continues to rise, but at a slower pace largely due to less favorable demographic factors, higher nominal interest rates, and the transfer of resources to the war machine. Stock prices also rise at a slower pace as interest rates begin to impact investment opportunities and as the rate of economic growth nears an upper limit.

The Fourth Decade - Transition and Stagnation

Although an aura of false security tends to occupy much of the fourth decade, it is rudely shocked towards the end of the period by sharply deteriorating economic, moral, and social conditions. The general mood of the electorate is towards the international area reflecting the nation's gain in worldwide stature in the previous decade.[6] After the hectic social issues, domestic unrest, and wars of the previous decade, the fourth decade is viewed as a period for "getting back to basics."

Monetary policy becomes very restrictive; and even though this period (as well as the fifth decade) is, on average, marked by declining prices, the inflationary pressures of the preceding decade are a major concern to monetary authorities. To slow price expectations they reduce the rate of money growth and, as a result, the productive capacity built during the war years

TABLE 3.4

Timing of Wholesale Price Increases During Kondratieff Cycles

Decade Since Depression	Wholesale prices
1st Decade	
1786-1795	+ 3.4%
1836-1845	− 2.8
1886-1895	− 1.5
1940-1949	+ 7.1
2nd Decade	
1796-1805	+ 0.2
1846-1855	+ 3.0
1896-1905	+ 2.1
1950-1959	+ 1.9
3rd Decade	
1806-1815	+ 2.1
1856-1865	+ 6.7
1906-1919	+ 6.1
1960-1969	+ 1.2
4th Decade	
1816-1825	− 4.8
1866-1875	− 4.7
1920-1929	− 3.7
1970-1979	+ 8.3
5th Decade	
1826-1835	− 0.2
1876-1885	− 3.4
1930-1939	− 2.1
1980-1989	N/A

Note: Wholesale prices given in average percent change per year

TABLE 3.5

Nation's Mood And Related Topics

	Nation's Mood	Foreign Trade	Political Scandals
1st Decade 1786-1795 1836-1845 1886-1895 1940-1949	Conservative	Protectionist	None
2nd Decade 1796-1805 1846-1855 1896-1905 1950-1959	Maximize Wealth	Free Trade	None
3rd Decade 1806-1815 1856-1865 1906-1919 1960-1969	Progressive/ Reform-Minded	Free Trade	None
4th Decade 1816-1825 1866-1875 1920-1929 1970-1979	International	Protectionist	Election of 1824 Carpetbaggers' Teapot Dome Watergate
5th Decade 1826-1835 1876-1885 1930-1939 1980-1989	Conservative	Extreme Protectionism	None

of the third decade becomes excessive. Thus, after three decades of accelerating growth, real economic activity slows sharply. The unemployment rate begins to rise as businesses cut costs in reaction to weak economic demand.

Contrary to the belief of many analysts and politicians, this decade's high real interest rates are not "unprecedented," but rather are actually a norm for this phase of the cycle. In contrast to the period 1945-1975, yes, today's real interest rates are very high. However, if one looks back to previous fourth decade periods (e.g. 1816-1825, 1866-1875, and the 1920s), one sees that high real interest rates are very common. Indeed, it is precisely the sharp swing from low to high real interest rates—a tremendous shock to the economic system—that sets into motion, over a period of many years, the processes which lead to depression.

Furthermore, as economic activity slows sharply, the nation becomes increasingly protectionistic which only serves to aggravate the economic growth problems and exacerbate inflationary pressures. Later, with the advent of retaliatory policies worldwide, it then impairs international trade and leads to prolonged economic stagnation.

Contradictions abound in the fourth decade. There is a surge in new patents which may one day bring stronger economic growth; but high interest rates, unavailable financial capital, weakening economic demand, a public not yet ready to accept the new products, and labor's resistance to any loss of jobs in the old growth industries, all block their practical application. Conversely, there is an outpouring of negative news events. But speculative bubbles of optimism pop up as people are fooled into thinking the current bad economic climate is just an aberration to be followed by rapid growth as observed in the earlier decades. There is a spurt in housing demand as the baby boom generation—born during the first decade when couples could afford to have families—reaches prime home-buying ages; but it merely leads to a further worsening of inflationary expectations and additional pressures on nominal and real interest rates. There are numerous land booms but, by the end of the fourth decade, construction activity is already plunging in reaction to the high real interest rates.

The underlying cause of these contradictions leads us back

to the concept of rational expectations: People become aware of the true long-run impact of rapid money growth and increasingly anticipate the inflationary consequences. Therefore, the money tends to be diverted towards get-rich-quick speculative ventures and higher prices rather than real output.

Meanwhile, the business failure rate surges. To most participants, the failures come as a shock. But they are the natural consequence of the first 40 years of the Kondratieff cycle—particularly the overexpansion of the third decade. Throughout those four decades, society increasingly acquired massive amounts of debt, expecting to pay it back in cheaper dollars. However, high real interest rates and falling commodity prices make debt servicing extremely expensive for individuals, businesses, and nations—so much so that many are forced to default. Thus, a decade that began on a very calm note ends with extremely negative overtones.

The Fifth Decade - Depression

The depression finally develops during the fifth decade. A highly restrictive monetary policy designed to prevent a price reacceleration causes real economic activity to spiral downward. Unemployment soars. Stock prices, housing activity, and commodity prices plunge. The resulting sharp decline in consumer wealth forces individuals to replenish their savings rather than spend. Even though nominal interest rates drop dramatically, inflation falls even more rapidly, thereby keeping real interest rates at a high level. Extreme protectionism causes a worldwide transmission of the depression as foreign trade falls; and the largely depreciated plant and equipment sit idle. Business investment collapses under the strain.

All these events lead to loan defaults and bank runs. To the degree the public withdraws deposits, they precipitate a string of bank failures and a potential collapse of the domestic and international financial systems, increasing dramatically the severity of the depression. Income declines feed back to reduce money growth, even further accelerating the economy's downward spiral. Finally, the process careens out of control when individuals, corporations, and nations lose all faith in the economic system, causing a sharp plunge in the demand for money and finally wiping out excess debts. The inflationary expectations of old are replaced by the deflationary fears of a new era.

The rapid economic decline and accompanying business failures weed out the nation's inefficient industries. The resulting deflation eventually puts to rest the Fed's fear of provoking hyperinflation, allowing the seeds for the next Kondratieff wave to be planted. Once convinced the long inflation battle is won, the Fed begins to spur economic activity. By pumping money into the economy again, deflation stops and mild inflation begins anew. The depression-induced plunge in nominal interest rates is now finally matched by a sharp drop in real interest rates—a key prerequisite to any revival in consumer spending, business investment, or the economy as a whole.

The rash of bankruptcies during the depression frees financial capital for young industries that are eager to supply the economy with new and innovative processes. Thus, the large surge in patents during the fourth decade can now reach the market although, initially, their impact is limited by poor economic conditions. A subset of these innovations, nevertheless, become the catalyst for rapid economic growth during the rising phase of the next long wave. In this way, the old, antiquated industrial base is replaced with a vibrant, cost-effective, and productive technical base.

Consequences of Disbelieving the Long Wave

Because most economists ignore the long wave hypothesis, their forecasts tend to overpredict real GNP and underpredict inflation, interest rates, and unemployment. Charts 3.1-3.4 compare most forecasters' viewpoint with the long wave and graphically depict the pitfalls of the conventional view.

Most implicitly assume the economy grows at a positive and slightly accelerating rate of growth over the long run, much as we have seen since 1945 (see chart 3.1). As a result, they invariably construct their economic models with data from the 1950s to the mid-1970s or early 1980s, using these data for their various mathematical formulas. They apply statistical techniques to the post WWII sample to find the line or growth path that best predicts the data for the available time period. They implicitly assume that the economic structure during the forecast horizon (the present and the future) is no different than that during the sample period (the past). But if this one assumption is wrong, it means that the entire complex of formulas is—without exception—also wrong.

In reality, the economy's growth rate changes in a predictable fashion during the 40-60 year Kondratieff cycle and, depending upon where the economy is in this cycle, economic variables react differently to apparently equivalent stimuli. Chart 3.2 depicts the long wave in recent years. The trough of the last complete long cycle occurred in the early 1930s. Then, late in that decade, the next cycle's long rising phase began, probably reaching its peak around 1965-1967 when the growth rate in productivity reached a peak and began to trend downward. A down phase has ensued since that point. If the long-wave theory is applied, then straight-line forecasting techniques—the basis for today's economic analysis—cannot be applied to the entire sample period. Indeed, as the time horizon is extended, the discrepancy resulting from straight-line projections yields larger and larger errors as shown in Chart 3.3.

In standard econometric models used by economists, a straight line is drawn in such a way as to minimize the difference between itself and the economy's actual path during the sample time period, in effect averaging out the entire period. Most economic forecasters utilize economic data back to the early 1950s. But since the bulk of the data refers to the economy's rising portion when we did enjoy rapid economic

CHART 3.1. TRADITIONAL VIEW OF THE U.S. ECONOMY

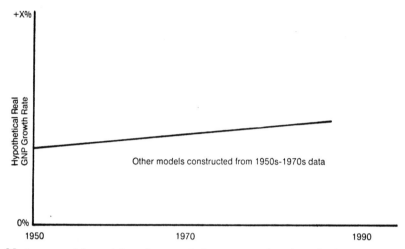

Most econometric models and economic forecasts are based on the long-run up-trend implicit in economic data from the 1950s to the present. Therefore, most assume the economy will continue to grow at a positive and slightly accelerating rate as time passes.

CHART 3.2. LONG-WAVE VIEW OF THE U.S. ECONOMY

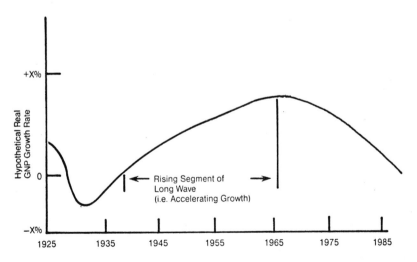

This book is based on an economic theory and econometric model which incorporates the 40-60 Kondratieff or long-wave cycle. In contrast to the traditional view, economic growth follows a wave pattern: (1) from depression, (2) to recovery, (3) to prosperity (4) to decelerating growth, and (5) back to a depression.

CHART 3.3. WHY MOST ECONOMIC FORECASTS GO ASTRAY

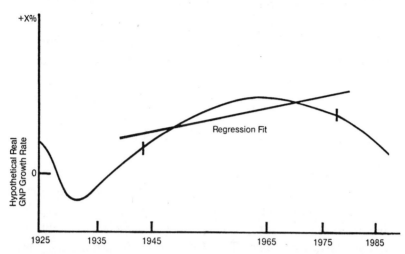

If standard straight-line economic forecasting techniques are applied to the entire 1950s-1980s period and if the long-wave process is the true view of the economy, then most economists will increasingly go awry in the 1980s—forecasting strong economic growth when an actual depression is developing.

CHART 3.4. CORRECTING THE BIAS IN MOST ECONOMIC FORECASTS

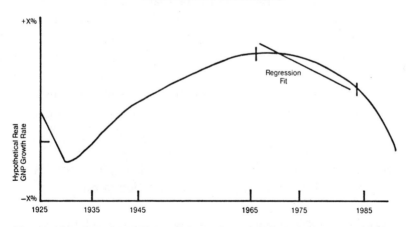

To correct the inaccuracy of current straight-line economic forecasting techniques, only a specific portion of the long wave should be used to generate a forecast. If we are in the downward leg of the Kondratieff cycle, as believed, then a new forecast line, using only those data, generates a more accurate projection.

growth with relatively low unemployment, interest rates, and inflation, it reflects too much of the distant history and too little of the economy's more recent past. As a result, they mistakenly extrapolate the long cycle's rising phase into the downward leg of the 1970s and 1980s. This is the reason for most forecasters' perpetually rosy forecasts—that a turn for the better is just around the corner. Unfortunately, their failure to take into account the overpowering effects of the Kondratieff wave means they will repeatedly experience large projection errors of the type discussed above.

The question is: How does a researcher build an economic model when detailed data are only available for three-fourths of one long cycle and when the economy is always changing? The solution is to apply the straight-line technique only over the cycle's down phase. The 1967 break in productivity provides the key insight as to when the cycle's rising phase stopped and the down phase began. As shown in Chart 3.4, the new line generates a more accurate forecast since it is applied to a segment of the long wave where the structure remains relatively stable throughout.

As discussed earlier, one of the key criticisms made by Keynesians of monetary theory is that, due to an unstable money/economy relationship, knowledge of money's past movement is useless in trying to forecast future economic activity or inflation. Using data from only one phase of the long wave to forecast a period within that same phase helps to counter this claim. Thus, the method reestablishes money as a powerful forecasting tool. However, it does not—and is not intended to—support the traditional monetarist belief that economic activity will be largely devoid of cycles if only money were supplied at a stable pace; or that the system is inherently stable save for the errant application of monetary policy.

Within my framework, the money/economy relationship is considered relatively stable only during individual up and down phases of the Kondratieff wave. Over the entire Kondratieff cycle, the money/economy relationship shifts violently.

Since the shift can be very abrupt, the solution adopted here is to base one's forecast on data only from the current phase in operation.

Thus, the straight-line technique is adapted to outperform conventional forecasters, given the long wave's existence. But even with this improvement, ever increasing forecast errors (although still much smaller than those of traditional economists) develop as the economy approaches a depression. The economic structure does not necessarily change in neatly segregated phases. Rather, it is constantly in flux throughout a long cycle. Moreover, any time the economy approaches a turning point—which more often than not is bound to be abrupt—the straight-line approach is invalidated, as all economic models generate larger and larger errors.

The economic tool most conducive to solving this problem is catastrophe theory. However, catastrophe theory is just in its infancy, with few mathematicians trained in its intricacies. And unlike the straight-line analysis, no standard computer programs exist for the theory's application to actual data.

> Scientists recognize two general kinds of processes in nature: continuous or "smooth" ones, such as the rotation of planets or the flow of electric current through a wire, and discontinuous or "abrupt" processes, which include such things as the sudden buckling of a girder under stress or the impulsive division of cells in growing tissue. The behavior of continuous processes can be understood by using calculus, invented by Isaac Newton and Gottfried Leibnitz 300 years ago. But there has never been an equally effective form of mathematics for explaining and predicting the occurrence of discontinuous phenomena. Now, however, as a result of recent work by Rene Thom, professor of mathematics at the Paris Institute for Higher Scientific Studies, such a theory is emerging....
>
> Thom's work is called "catastrophe theory" because it describes phenomena (not necessarily disasters) that jump abruptly from one form of behavior to a radically different one.[7]

Prior to the advent of catastrophe theory, no mathematical

justification could be used to explain depressions. A depression, as such, is a "discontinuity." It does not fit into the smooth and continuous assumptions behind straight-line economic techniques that permeate the science of economics as a whole. Economic theories are dependent on the mathematical tools available in order to formulate, test, and prove various hypotheses. If the tools only allow continuous events, then the economic theory, too, is forced to assume only continuous events, leaving depressions as an unexplained oddity.

In other words, economic theory today is handcuffed by the very restrictions and unrealistic assumptions present in straight-line mathematical forecasting tools. But the real world does not operate in a straight-line fashion. Rather, such discontinuous phenomena as repeated depressions, speculative booms and sudden busts are a fact of life.

Chart 3.5 depicts the Kondratieff cycle through catastrophe theory analysis. In the first decade following the previous depression, real GNP (Y1) is expanding but from a low level. The greatest real GNP growth occurs during the third decade (point 3) as the economy moves from the lower fold to the upper fold. During the fourth decade, however, inflationary pressures and expectations become a dominant force, leading policymakers to accept slower rates of real GNP growth to prevent hyperinflation.

The inflationary constraint then causes the economic system to fall back, collapsing on itself, much as a star explodes and then implodes, creating a black hole. The exit from the depression is, in effect, into another universe—a new long wave. In both cases the system is squeezed or made more efficient before the next cycle proceeds.

The Fed's inability, for example, to allow rapid money growth to spur real economic activity to an ever higher section of the upper fold—in order to prevent rampant inflation and strong inflationary expectations—causes real GNP to fall back into the fold at point 4 causing the catastrophic plunge to point 5 during the fifth decade. The catastrophe could be

**CHART 3.5. EXPLAINING A DEPRESSION THROUGH
CATASTROPHE THEORY**

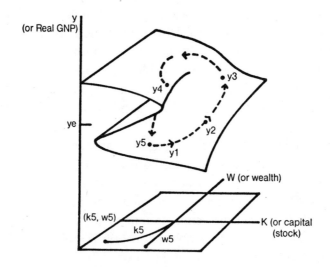

Only the advanced mathematical approach—catastrophe theory— accurately represents the full expanse of the long-wave cycle. By definition, current economic theories and tools cannot account for the "catastrophic" plunge of a depression from points 4 to 5. Unfortunately, however, catastrophe theory is so new, it is not readily available to solve economic problems at this time.

caused by a sharp drop in wealth, perhaps due to an oil price collapse which precipitates a stock market crash, massive individual, corporate, and national failures. The failures, in turn, cause the capital stock to shrink to a very low level following the depressionary collapse. Then, the cycle starts over again.

Why The Depression Can't Be Prevented

Solutions to the 1930s depression are implicit in Keynesian, supply-side, and monetarist theories. However, there are several reasons why these prescriptions will not be successful in preventing a 1980s depression.

The Fallacy of the Keynesian Solution

For the Keynesian depression solution to work in the 1980s, a massive Government spending spree funded by the Federal Reserve would be needed. However, if the Fed fails to provide the monetary stimulus, the private and public sectors clash in a battle for available funds, pushing interest rates higher and further aggravating economic conditions; and even if the Fed supported the fiscal stimulus, a massive inflationary bulge would quickly develop.

The causes for this impasse transcend the traditional Keynesian-monetarist debate. Late in a long cycle, real potential economic growth is stymied by the antiquated plant and equipment base, protectionism, high real interest rates, highly imbedded inflationary expectations, and overall uncertainty. Thus, the economy is unable to sustain a rapid rate of growth without generating rampant inflation. The massive money infusion that is required by the Fed to overcome these obstacles and to forestall the depression with a low interest rate environment, leads to a sharp price acceleration which eventually degenerates into depression anyway.

The Keynesian explanation of the 1930s depression is lacking in several critical areas. Since nominal interest rates fell to such low levels, Keynesians argue that monetary policy was very expansionary and that, despite this so-called easy money, the economy remained in a depression. This demonstrated, in their view, that money and monetary policy was always unimportant. But declining nominal interest rates are not the definitive sign of easier Fed policy. Rather, the indicators to watch are: (a) real interest rates and (b) the rate of money growth relative to the nation's productivity trend. In the 1920s, the Fed maintained a tight monetary policy to control inflation and, thus, over the years high real interest rates accentuated the problems of an aging capital base. Even if there was a desire to undertake a massive switch from the aging capital industries to the new growth industries, the necessary financing was prohibitively expensive in inflation-adjusted terms. Thus, in contrast to the Keynesian picture, very restrictive monetary policy was a key factor in precipitating and sustaining the Depression. However, as will be pointed out in subsequent paragraphs, no matter how powerful monetary policy might be, it could not have indefinitely forestalled the collapse.

Contrary to the Keynesian view, the Fed could have been vastly more accommodating in the late 1920s and early 1930s and probably could have reduced the sharpness of the collapse. Proof of this is provided in Milton Friedman's and Anna Schwartz' *Monetary History of the United States.* In early 1932, the Fed undertook a large-scale operation to flood the banking system with money—its only overt stimulative move during the Depression. Whereas previous interest rate declines were due simply to falling economic demand and declining loan activity, this time, however, the Fed was actively forcing rates down. Within 5-6 months, major economic indicators, such as income, production, and employment began to rise—a time lag consistent with monetarist analysis. Thus, if the Fed had continued their expansionary policy, the Depression could have been halted at that time. The consequence, however, would have been an inflationary surge.[8]

Although monetary policy was the most important factor leading to the 1930s depression, it was not the only one. Other real economic phenomena also contributed to the Depression's severity: Overinvestment in the capital goods industry earlier in the long wave led to a collapse in investment opportunities. Antiquated production processes necessitated protectionist policies to prevent domestic producers from losing their markets to cheaper foreign competition. The stock market crash and the 1925-1930 housing collapse seriously eroded consumer wealth, forcing consumers to switch from spending to saving. Corporate failures eventually resulted as companies were unable to service the massive debt they had accumulated over the years. Loan defaults caused bank failures and further downward pressure on money growth. In summary, the Keynesian solution needed the assistance of monetary policy to prevent the Depression. However, monetary policy's impotency late in a long cycle allowed the collapse to proceed unabated.

The Fallacy of the Supply-Sider Solution

A more recent theoretical solution for depressions is presented by supply-side economists who recommend tax cuts (in effect, an expansionary fiscal policy) to boost investment in combination with a gold-backed U.S. dollar. In their view, this insures the desired economic growth. But they underestimate the need for the monetary authorities to support the fiscal policy moves—precisely the opposite of what they would normally get by going to the highly restrictive monetary policy implied by the gold standard. In a depression and under a gold standard, private investors tend to bypass domestic ventures in favor of higher yielding foreign investments. As capital flows out of the country, the receiving nation demands gold from the U.S. for the dollars it receives which, in turn, causes a drain on U.S. money growth. Since, under a strict gold standard, the Federal Reserve cannot offset the drain, this mechanism actually intensifies the developing economic collapse. And if the rules of the gold standard are not followed, then monetary policy becomes very expansionary, leading to rampant inflation.

The Fallacy of the Monetarist Solution

The monetary view presented by Friedman and Schwartz is that the Fed could have significantly reduced the Depression's severity by continuing massive money pumping operations similar in magnitude to that of 1932; and that it should have continued until the economy had recovered. However, a fatal flaw in monetary policy effectively prevents the Federal Reserve from reversing the depression—namely that, late in a long cycle, it is rendered virtually impotent by the inflationary psychology stemming from earlier rapid money growth. Thus, during the 1920s and 1930s, the Fed kept a tight reign on money for a good reason—the fear of invoking a sharp inflation acceleration.[9]

What would have occurred in the 1930s if the Fed did indeed implement a massive expansionary program? Keynesians and monetarists believe the tremendous excess capacity at that time would have prevented an inflation acceleration. However, Friedman and Schwartz' own research proves otherwise. The large scale money infusion of April 1932 is, in effect, a controlled experiment in monetary policy. And, just as Friedman and Schwartz themselves use that period to show how the Fed could have significantly boosted economic activity, the same period can also be used to show how inflation would have accelerated dramatically.

It is important to note that 1932 is considered by some to be the Depression's trough or possibly one of two bottoms (with the other in 1933). At such times, inflationary pressures should be at their weakest. But despite being at one of the Depression's lowest points, the large Fed money pumping operation actually led to a very sharp change in the inflation rate shortly after the Fed action. Wholesale prices—which had declined at a 12.1% annual clip from March 1931 through June 1932 and by 14.9% from December 1931 through March 1932—suddenly turned around and began to actually rise by July of 1932, only three months after the April money infusion. If the money infusion had continued, a sharp inflationary surge would have developed.

To believe the Fed has the power to prevent depressions, one must carry monetarism to an extreme—accept the notion that only money matters and that there is no factor inhibiting the Fed's use of money to stabilize the economy. In actuality, monetary policy is trapped at key periods by its own sheer power as psychology and inflationary fears dominate both the financial markets and the Fed itself.

Towards the end of a long wave, many factors come

together. Due to a tight monetary policy, high real interest rates prevent new plant and equipment investment. Thus, the old industrial base just keeps getting older and more inefficient, requiring ever larger doses of money to compensate for the system's inefficiency and to sustain the previous level of economic growth. Inflationary pressures build rapidly. Money growth could be boosted significantly in the short run with desired effects of spurring economic activity and lowering unemployment. But in the longer run, the far more powerful consequence—high inflation and a complete reversal of the initial real economic gains—becomes obvious to everyone. As the long wave inches ever closer to its end, economic participants become increasingly conscious of the power of money—and painfully aware of its scarcity as distress borrowing and corporate bankruptcies begin to surface. The Fed fears a massive money infusion will induce a surge in inflation which will have to be corrected at a subsequent date by reversing any money infusions initially undertaken. At the same time, the marketplace finally senses deflation is brewing and reduces spending on goods and services in favor of saving through short-term securities.

This massive shift in expectations and the subsequent crisis in business confidence brings on a complete breakdown in the money/economy relationship, causing a sharp price drop in key assets such as oil, housing, stocks, and bonds; and it is this wealth erosion which makes monetary policy impotent. To offset the economic plunge, the Fed would have to pump a massive amount of money into the banking system precisely when underlying inflationary expectations and pressures are already intense. In short, inflationary expectations become the Achilles' heel of monetary policy. Monetary policy's power to boost both the economy and inflation are so widely recognized that the time lag between action and reaction shrinks dramatically, trapping the Fed in its own vice and eventually forcing it to take the deflationary path.

This dramatic shrinkage of time lags is the most critical characteristic of the long wave's late stage. Normally the time lag between a money pumping campaign and its impact on prices is one and a half years. But as indicated above, in the 1930s, it was a mere three months. Similarly, throughout the first 35 years of the long wave, a surge in the money supply did not adversely affect bond markets until after the inflationary consequences became apparent. Now, bond markets react immediately—long before the money impacts the economy.

4

The World Supremacy
Cycle

Before a definitive portrait of the future economic landscape can be painted, one must recognize the very long-range economic, social, and political problems and/or constraints that are superimposed on our next 40-60 year cycle. This chapter addresses these very long-range issues while, at the same time, proving the existence and validity of the long wave itself.

Milton Friedman and Anna Schwartz in their book *Monetary Trends of the United States and the United Kingdom* reject the long-swing hypothesis because concurrent depressions in the U.S. and the United Kingdom from 1867 were so different in magnitude. They imply that, if the long wave were valid, it should generate depressions of equal intensity in the same time period for both countries since Britain and the U.S. are so similar in so many other ways. But not finding such regularity, they conclude that the long swings do not represent repeating or self-generating cycles, but rather are produced by random wars and random depressions which are particular to each nation.[10]

The Friedman-Schwartz analysis does not take into account

the economic and political supremacy cycle. Their data begin with England's second long wave as a world leader after which a milder depression is typical, simply because following the earlier depression, institutions and laws were established which tended to minimize the downward flight of the long wave. The aftereffect, however, was a highly imbedded inflation and inflationary psychology. In other words, the 1940-1989 U.S. period corresponds to England's 1836-1885 era.

In both countries, the first fifty years of the economic supremacy cycle were characterized by a public which was relatively unaware of the power of monetary policy, allowing money growth to generate larger changes in real output relative to prices. In the second (and to an even greater degree during the third) long wave of the supremacy cycle, money growth is largely anticipated leading to higher inflation relative to real economic growth. Thus, society becomes very conscious of monetary forces, adjusting their expectations in a rational manner after experiencing the severe depression of the first long wave within the supremacy cycle.

Britain's first long wave during their 150-year supremacy cycle (i.e. 1836-1885) corresponds to America's first long wave of 1890-1939 during our supremacy cycle. And, in turn, the second British cycle of the 1836-1885 period is equivalent to our second long wave of 1940-1989. Since the U.S. is on a different plane of the economic supremacy cycle, concurrent U.S. and English depressions are naturally different. But by moving England's history forward by 100 years, the regular patterns which Friedman and Schwartz felt were largely absent now become apparent.

Up to now, the long wave was assumed to be static or unchanging in that the patterns occur in a regular way with each and every 40-60 cycle. But just as the previous chapter showed how the normal 3-5 year business cycle changes over the course of a long wave, this chapter reveals how the Kondratieff cycle changes over a nation's 150-year world supremacy cycle.

The key factor which alters the long wave from cycle to cycle is the degree of direct Governmental intervention through large deficits and social welfare nets. Much as England attempted to defuse the long wave in a comparable period 100-150 years ago by building safety nets and institutions to prevent a repeat of their massive depression of the 1830s, we have made similar attempts to prevent a recurrence of the 1930s plunge. And much as England was unable to prevent its next depression, managing instead only to reduce its severity, we can expect a similar situation will develop.

However, there are key differences between our situation now and England's comparable period 100 years ago. Prices, interest rates, and other important statistics have soared over the past fifty years at a much more rapid pace than previous eras. For example, in 1814, the U.S. wholesale price index stood at 58.7. In 1945—over 130 years later—it still was at about the same level, or 55.2. But since 1945, prices have risen by a factor of about five and a half times. Has the worldwide Governmental intervention through the implementation of Keynesian fiscal policies caused a permanent and fundamental change in the long wave?

The structural change that has occurred since the last depression is real and is directly related to Germany's 1922-23 hyperinflation and the supremacy cycle. As was discussed in greater detail earlier, the German hyperinflation led to an environment where an Adolf Hitler could come to power. Hitler's emergence precipitated World War II which was a war that did not accurately fit into the long wave's normal sequence of events. Thus, World War II cut short the economic stagnation and housecleaning that usually occur in the first decade following a depression. With inflationary pressures not sufficiently eradicated during the 1930s and with demand pressures of a war in the 1940s, inflation quickly accelerated unlike previous cycles. These events imply a mammoth depression would be necessary to fully correct the higher level of world inflation today.

The structural change also relates to the world's combined

attempt to soften the blow or reduce the magnitude of the Kondratieff cycle. The Western nations as a whole have built large safety nets and have heavily relied on Governmental intervention during the past 50 years. When recessions develop, market forces are impeded by Governmental actions. The result is that a thorough cleansing of excessive debt, inventories, and inflation is not accomplished. To the degree market forces are impeded, inflationary pressures tend to remain intact.

This concerted worldwide effort to avert a 1930s-type depression has resulted in an increasingly socialistic infrastructure, which may reduce the severity of the long wave's depression. But it also limits the upward potential of the next long wave. Moreover, these economic restrictions reflect equivalent limitations to the individuals' freedom to speculate or to freely choose products and investments. So the issue is to what degree will Western nations be more or less socialistic in future years. To eliminate our deep inflation legacy, a massive depression is necessary. But political pressures block the full extent of such a decline. Thus, Western nations are evolving into socialistic economies much as England has since the 1930s.

The extreme of this trend is the Soviet Union. By strictly controlling human behavior, the Russian economy largely avoids or greatly reduces the relative impact of a worldwide depression. To avoid the large ups and downs, the Russians, in effect, have a permanent depressionary period through extreme social control. But in order to do so, increasingly repressive actions are undertaken. So a continually evolving world political system may be occurring where the Soviet Union eventually tilts more towards capitalism to soothe the increasing social unrest resulting from Russia's poor standard of living; while Western nations turn more socialistic by using controls to reduce the amplitude of economic swings. The long wave can be modified, but at a very heavy price—the loss of economic and social freedoms.

Throughout Western history following the dark ages, one

nation has typically been the world economic and political leader over roughly a 150-year span or, on average, for three Kondratieff cycles.

The first of the three long waves is when the transfer of leadership occurs between the current but weakening world power and the newly emerging supreme nation. By the middle to the end of this first long wave, the old world power is supplanted by the new one. But the rising star is like an inexperienced lover who must first learn by costly mistakes; this first fifty years of the supremacy cycle culminates in a depression that is typically the most devastating the country sees. However, precisely because it is so severe, a total housecleaning is accomplished, permitting strong economic growth during the second 50-year period of the supremacy cycle.

The second 50-year long wave within the 150-year supremacy cycle is when the new world leader solidifies its position through trade and wealth accumulation, as well as through the accompanying political influence and power. The long wave's upward phase during this period is usually viewed as a golden age, whereas the declining mode is seen as a nightmare of broken dreams and disappointments. Although psychologically devastating, in concrete forms, the depression of the second cycle is not as severe as the first depression because memory of that first devastating collapse causes the nation to establish social safety nets, bureaucracies, and company bail-outs that limit the next major plunge. But, in so doing, imbedded inflationary pressures are not totally eradicated, and the nation accepts a higher rate of inflation going into the third long wave. Companies that should have failed in the second depression do not.

As a result, in the third and last long wave of the nation's supremacy cycle, the availability of financial capital for industries with new innovative processes is not as abundant as it was in the second. With the higher, built-in inflation and with fewer innovative processes able to come on board, growth potential is very limited. The leading nation's economy begins to stagnate and a new world leader begins to emerge as the 150-

year old world master succumbs to the new nation's powers, vitality, and economic promise. By the end of the third long wave of the supremacy cycle, the old master evolves into an inflation-ruined and socialist nation that is no match for the new leader; and the mantle of world supremacy is officially transferred during this period, typically through a direct or indirect war. Although the old power retains a voice in world and economic events after this, it is now reduced to a second-rate power—unable to support its position without considerable help from its allies.

The Regularity of Wars

As Table 4.1. shows, this "changing of the guard" has been quite regular over the past 350 years. Moreover, the transition has consistently taken place with major wars all occurring in the third decade of the leading nation's third long wave of its supremacy cycle. The table shows that, in each case, the old world power is dethroned during its third Kondratieff wave of its supremacy cycle, whereas the newly emerging power establishes its claim during its own first long wave of its cycle. As a result, the period roughly 100 years earlier for the dethroned leader corresponds to the conditions for the current new economic power.

The War of Spanish Succession developed in Spain's third long wave of its supremacy cycle, culminating its long-term decline that was already well under way and removing any doubts that France was the new world leader. Then, in the early 1800s, it was France's turn to relinquish its power in Napoleon's defeat by the British at Waterloo. As with Spain, by the time of its defeat, France had already been weakened by the French revolution and hyperinflation of the late 1700s which greatly sapped the economy's wealth and creativity. Waterloo confirmed the end.

In contrast, the rise of the United States was not via direct aggression with the previous world power. Rather, during

TABLE 4.1

"Changing of the Guard" via "Third Decade" Wars

During Past Economic Supremacy Cycles

	Spain	France	England	U.S.
Cycle's First Long Wave	War With Portugal	War of Spanish Succession	Battle of Waterloo	WWI
(decade)	1606-1619	1706-1719	1806-1819	1906-1919
Cycle's Third Long Wave	War of Spanish Succession	Battle of Waterloo	WWI	Hypothesized War
(decade)	1710-1719	1810-1819	1910-1919	2010-2019

World War I, when the U.S. replaced Britain as the dominant economic force, the two nations were allies. However, England's inability to win the war without U.S. assistance marked the end of Britain's reign as the weight of America's muscle defeated Germany—another possible contender for England's supremacy position. Regardless of the specific events, however, in each case, the general pattern is the same: The younger nation (in its first long wave of its supremacy cycle) usurps the previous world power (in its third long wave of its supremacy cycle), with major wars during each nation's third decade from the last depression.

These wars—considered by Friedman and Schwartz to be random events which then precipitate the randomness of depressions—are themselves events which occur with marked regularity. Thus, by showing the regularity of wars and the predictability of the world power structure that emerges, the first of Friedman and Schwartz's conditions to confirm the validity of a regular long wave is met.

The second requirement is to show that the relative severity of each depression in each phase of the past four supremacy cycles is also regular.

The Regularity of Depressions

When analyzing the timing and severity of past depressions, one is forced to rely on descriptive historical accounts to ascertain economic conditions. Unfortunately, reliable economic data are not available for much of the 400-year expanse of the past four supremacy cycles. What data are available, however, are used.

Table 4.2. highlights the hypothesized depressionary times for the past four supremacy cycles. The depressions that are similar in magnitude between different world leaders should fall approximately 100 years apart.

To meet the final test of the Friedman-Schwartz challenge as to the existence of repeating long waves, economic history should show evidence of depressionary conditions during the approximate periods cited above; and, furthermore, each depression across a particular supremacy cycle (i.e. from country to country) should exhibit declines of approximately equal severity or at least follow a predictable pattern. If evidence proves that these depressions did indeed occur and that they occurred to the degree predicted from the initial U.S. dating scheme, then the Kondratieff cycle should be accepted as a confirmed hypothesis—not merely a theory or fiction.

Depressions of the First Long Wave

The four depressions of the first long wave of the supremacy cycle occurred in Spain of the 1630s, France of the 1730s, England of the 1830s, and United States of the 1930s. In each case, the depressions were preceded by rapid money growth—either via precious metal inflows or the unbounded creation of paper money—which led to rapid inflation and

TABLE 4.2.

Hypothesized Depressions for Past Supremacy Cycles

(U.S. depression record initializes the dating basis)

Long Wave Within The Supremacy Cycle	Spain	France	England	U.S.
1st	1630-1639	1730-1739	1830-1839	1930-1939
2nd	1680-1689	1780-1789	1880-1889	1980-1989
3rd	1730-1739	1830-1839	1930-1939	2030-2039

strong inflationary fears. And, in each case, severe monetary restraint to correct rapid inflation precipitated the depression and resulting deflation.

> At frequent intervals in the last three-quarters of the 17th century (for Spain), the evils of inflation called forth corrective deflation, with sharp declines in the commodity price level and severe commercial crises as inevitable consequences. The deflationary decree of 1628 brought prices downward by 9 per cent.[11]

Spain's economic carnage continued until the early 1640s with periods of sharp inflation quickly reversed by longer periods of rapid deflation. Following Spain's defeat of Portugal, the previous world leader, Spain never effectively consolidated its power throughout its supremacy cycle. However, as will be noted in subsequent paragraphs, later world economic powers were successful in doing so, which implies a dynamic or changing character to the supremacy cycle as well. The first major depression as a world leader left Spain in a relatively less desirable position than her counterparts in the second long wave of the supremacy cycle.

The French depression of 1730-1739 was also a relatively weak cleansing out of the economic system. Since the depression was not as severe as it should have been, inflationary pressures were never adequately quelled.

As compared to Spain and France, the English depression of 1830-1839 was very sharp, putting her in a much better position to forge ahead in the second long wave of her supremacy cycle. Thus, the "earlier overexpansion of the cotton mills resulted in a terrible period of depression; a period that was called England's creative destruction."[12] Various accounts place the timing of this depression from 1825 until 1847.[13] So, in effect, the economic ramifications were quite prolonged, although just as in the 1929-1939 period in the U.S., there were some intermittent upturns and rallies. But out of the sharp depression, there emerged England's golden period which began in the early 1840s and lasted until Britain's second depression as a world economic leader in the 1870s and 1880s.

The first U.S. depression during its world economic supremacy cycle was the 1930-1939 collapse. Obviously the deep housecleaning set the stage for the extremely prosperous period that has followed.

Consequently, a massive economic decline in the first 50-year period of a supremacy cycle generates a "golden age" in the succeeding growth period as the world leader solidifies its power base. And also observed is that, since the Spanish and French first depressions of their supremacy cycles were relatively mild, their subsequent economic recoveries and world influence were also relatively weaker, never quite reaching the same degree of strength as those later achieved by England and the U.S. in their second cycles. In this respect, the world supremacy cycle itself appears to be evolving towards more dramatic and traumatic first depressions, resulting in much stronger world leaders.

Depressions of the Second Long Wave

Included in the second supremacy cycle are the four depressionary periods of 1680-1689 for Spain, 1780-1789 for France,

1880-1889 for England, and the projected 1980-1989 period for the U.S.

The 1680-1689 Spanish depression appears to have been rather massive.[14] Since Spain did not incur a sharp depression in its first cycle, inflation problems became severe by the time of the second depression. Consequently the second depression was more severe as a thorough housecleaning was in order.

A national deficit problem of significant proportions invariably develops during a world leader's second long wave within its supremacy cycle. A combination of social safety nets and military operations leads to a guns-and-butter surge in Government spending. But tax increases are not rapid enough relative to expenditures, leading to a gaping deficit, a massive money pumping to finance it and, finally, sharply higher inflation.

Because of the bureaucracy and the built-in safety nets constructed in response to the first depression, a thorough liquidation of the debt or inflation excesses is not achieved; and because a firm foundation is not set following the second depression, the seeds for a strong third long-wave period in the supremacy cycle are not present. Companies that should be liquidated are patched up. Debts that should be repaid are papered over with still further debt extensions or rescheduling. The result is a deflation that is less rapid and less thorough in its cleansing of the imbedded inflationary pressures than was the case of the first one. Venture capital for new innovative processes is not as abundant as it was following the first depression, with too many antiquated companies using up scarce financial resources just to stay afloat as society, business, and politics militate against outright liquidations. By definition, this resistance to deep-going change limits the growth potential of the third long wave of the supremacy cycle and is the direct cause of many of the third long wave's most negative features.

The French depressionary period of 1780-1789 provides a classical case of Herculean efforts to prevent or cushion the depression—uncontrolled money creation to stave off economic collapse. The end result was first hyperinflation, destroying the wealth of the middle classes and second, depression, subjecting the French economy to a massive whipsaw which economic and political institutions were unable to withstand. Therein lies the seeds of the French Revolution, a totally new form of Government, and the rise of Napoleon whose first order of business was to shut down the printing presses and stop the hyperinflation.[15]

France's second depressionary period is the epitome of the massive chaos generated when attempting to fight the inevitable depression at any cost. Most people suffering through a depression see that 15-25% of the labor force may be unemployed. They fail to recognize that 75-85% of the labor force does continue to work. Thus, in a normal depression, the wealth and backbone of the middle class is not destroyed—it is merely damaged. And, although it does bring human suffering of alarming dimensions, it is still significantly less severe than the pain wrought by hyperinflation which first destroys the currency of the nation along with the wealth of all classes and then, on top of that, hits them with the depressionary conditions. Without the support, wealth, and stability of the middle class, existing political and social structures have no hope of surviving, and some form of revolution is guaranteed. The historical lesson is that those who want to prevent depressions by continually pumping more money into the economy would merely be setting the stage for the very destruction of the social and economic way of life that they are trying to protect.

Although the accelerating money infusion delayed France's second depression until the 1790s and early 1800s, the depression was still close to the timing scheme depicted throughout this book. Moreover, the processes at work to produce the depression were present at the hypothesized time, while only political intervention delayed its full arrival.

Of the many actual depressions recorded and reviewed over the past 400 years for Spain, France, England, and the U.S., only two periods involved severe hyperinflations to forestall the collapse. In a later chapter the causes of hyperinflations are explored in relation to the long-range U.S. forecast; and the patterns followed during the French and German hyperinflations are used to determine the possibility of such a debacle in the U.S. in future years.

Probably the most noteworthy impact of the second 50-year period depressions lies in the fact that they shatter the dreams and overconfidence that develop early in the second long wave. During the first and third long waves respectively, the world leader is first fighting to win its position and then reconciled to losing its throne. But throughout much of the second 50-year period of the supremacy cycle, the world leader is undeniably the dominant force in world events and builds up extreme self confidence from which any fall is psychologically devastating.

Possibly in reaction to the hyperinflation experiences, it appears that political forces of this middle period are trending towards relatively less extreme attempts to ward off the inevitable depression, resorting, instead, to a more indirect cushioning of the decline.

The 1870s-1880s English depression shows an evolution in Government and business savvy to artificially keep many technically defunct companies afloat. This is unlike the sharp vertical drop in Spain's second depression or France's socially destructive and undisciplined application of monetary policy in the 1790s. In effect, the English depression, although severe, is more fine-tuned both relative to past English depressions and to earlier second cycle depressions of Spain and France. The worst of the British depression occurred during the 1874-1879 period with a 9.2% drop in production of consumer goods and services. After an initial recovery, another slump developed in the early 1880s.[16]

The consumer panic—usually the most difficult to control—seemed to have been kept in check. Throughout the early phases, few recognized what was happening, as is human nature. Much as today, English forecasters in the second half of the 1800s painted a rosy picture—that events would turn for the better at any moment; and with each brief recovery during the drawn-out downward slide, this feeling or hope repeatedly surfaced.[17]

But the long decline sapped England's ingenuity and preeminence as the sole world power. As a result, she entered her third 50-year period of the supremacy cycle ill-prepared for military threats from Germany and unable to maintain her former dominant role in world markets as the U.S. entered the scene. The lack of massive liquidations (and the concurrent freeing-up of financial capital) hampered modernization. Consequently, the English industrial base became outdated,, resulting in higher priced and less efficient products and, finally, in England's loss of the economic marketplace.

In sum, the English 1870s-1880s depression was more like a soft landing relative to Spain's and France's second downturns within their supremacy cycles. Although the depression was still sharp in a statistical sense, its more devastating impact was on the high expectations that prevailed prior to the economic woes.[18] Individuals, businesses, and Government all found themselves downward revising their future expectations as the basic industries wallowed in stagnation, export markets vanished or were never fully recaptured, and worldwide trade protectionism set in.

In addition, social responsibilities to the electorate now took a larger and larger piece of the nation's total economic pie. To the degree one consumes past profits rather than reinvesting them to stay one step ahead of the competition, the competition will indeed match, and then overtake, previous market strongholds. Such was the fate of England beginning 100 years ago. If the similarities between then and now seem great, they should. Our depression in the 1980s should resemble the downturn of the British 1870s and 1880s.

Depressions of the Third Long Wave

The third long wave of the supremacy cycle contains the three depressionary eras of 1730-1739 for Spain, 1830-1839 for France, and 1930-1939 for England. By the time these depressions unfold, each country's role has been reduced to a second-rate power. In addition, the encrusted bureaucratic institutions and social safety nets make these depressions even milder than the ones experienced fifty years earlier. Again, the cost is high: deeply imbedded inflationary structure makes it impossible for the nation to do anything but stagnate during the third long wave, leading to its demise as a world leader.

The preceding paragraphs show that depressions—like wars—have occurred with clockwork regularity. In addition, with only limited exceptions, the relative severity of each cycle's depressions is roughly similar. Finally, the dynamic nature of the economic and political supremacy cycle itself also emerges. It appears that each succeeding depression in the first and third long waves is becoming more severe, while the second long wave's depression is becoming milder. The logic for this is probably that an increasingly interlocked and market-oriented economic system catches the new power by surprise in the first depression, making its severity that much worse because it is being compounded by the many international trade feedbacks. During the second 50-year period, the world leader is more in control of its own destiny and institutes progressively more sophisticated devices. This is presumably to prevent a future depression as the more recent leaders display greater abilities to fine tune monetary and fiscal policy, and as socialistic measures such as unemployment and health insurance have become more widespread over the centuries.

The depression of the third long wave, rather than being under the control of the now aging world leader, is actually influenced more by the emerging power's economic blunders and naivete. Meanwhile, with a more closely linked world economy, the third depression—although still less severe relative to the first and second downturns—is becoming increasingly more severe as we move from one 150-year cycle to the next.

What It Takes To Be The World's Supreme Power

It is during the pre-supremacy period that the prerequisites for becoming the dominant world leader are defined; a handful of key characteristics common to all past and current leaders generally develop in the two or three long waves leading up to the supremacy cycle.

First and foremost is independence—the elimination of any direct foreign influences—generally requiring a revolution much as the U.S. experienced in 1776-1783.

Second is agricultural self-sufficiency. No nation can expect to be the world power if it has to go begging for food.

Third, internal conflicts that impede a unified social and economic direction must be resolved, typically with a civil war which allows industrialists to win dominance over less progressive agricultural interests. Although agriculture remains important, it is the industrial war machine that speeds the development towards world supremacy, pushing forward the process at a fast and uninterrupted pace.

Fourth, the nation must be somewhat isolated or removed geographically from the center of world events, providing the natural protection and opportunity to develop without disruptions.

Fifth, during this pre-supremacy period, extensive land acquisitions and a widening sphere of influence must not be blocked by the then-world leader or by other powerful nations which view such action as (a) basically outside their area of interest, (b) effectively beyond their reach militarily, and/or (c) of secondary concern relative to more pressing matters. This land aquisition also allows the developing nation to build up and perfect its military with little interference from others.

The sixth major feature appears to be an evolution towards free trade or capitalistic tendencies. The capitalist approach will later tend to take on more socialistic overtones as the world leader matures and ages. But to achieve that initial thrust to world economic dominance, an increasingly capitalistic approach appears to be evolving from one supremacy cycle to the next, naturally necessitating more individual rights and stronger entrepreneurial forces. Throughout much of the supremacy cycle's first long wave, this entrepreneurism leads to innovative new processes, significantly boosting the nation's productive capacity and overall wealth. But carried to an extreme, it leads to speculative booms which, in turn, also breed speculative busts, causing depressions which are becoming more and more severe during the first and third long waves of the supremacy cycle. Apparently, progressively stronger individualistic and capitalistic tendencies are needed to spark sufficient energy and wealth to propel the newcomer to world power. But it is also when this speculative trait runs wild that a very massive housecleaning in the supremacy cycle's first long wave develops.

TABLE 4.3

World Economic and Political Supremacy Cycle Generalizations

Supremacy Stage	Generalization
Pre-Supremacy Cycles	Philosophical basis of nation established (e.g. Magna Carta, Articles of Confederation by the First Congress, Das Kapital/Communist Manifesto); land acquisitions at accelerating rate; revolutionary wars; civil wars; establishment of industrial and trade base; advanced agricultural methods; efficient and strong military complex.
Long Wave #1 of Supremacy Cycle	Old world leader (now weakened and in its third long wave of its supremacy cycle) is replaced by new leader (in its first long wave of its supremacy cycle) via direct or indirect war in third decade. Deep depression experienced by new world leader at end of current long wave.
Long Wave #2 of Supremacy Cycle	A golden era develops; power and wealth is unmatched by any other nation; world leader builds bureaucracy and implements social safety nets to soften depression which eventually leads to the world leader's demise.
Long Wave #3 of Supremacy Cycle	Highly imbedded inflationary pressures and massive Government deficits prevent the world leader from keeping up with new technological changes; internal pressures for Government aid to promote social welfare steals resources from research and development. Old power replaced by new, vibrant and economically more efficient nation.
Post-Supremacy Cycles	Socialism becomes intense, with high taxes; nation falls to second rate power; in many subsequent long waves, the socialization process weakens the nation to such a degree that it becomes a backward and poverty-stricken nation.

5

———

The 1980s Depression—Four Scenarios

The previous chapters establish the opportunities and constraints under which the U.S. economy and political system operate during the next 60 years. The following chapters forecast expected economic, social, and political conditions by decade, just as has been the pattern in previous discussions on the long wave and the world economic supremacy cycle. Obviously, when referring to the very near term, a much more detailed forecast can be made. Further out, the projection becomes more general.

The United States experiences its second depression as a world economic leader during the 1980s—just as past world economic leaders experienced depressions at this very juncture of their supremacy cycles and just as the U.S. itself has experienced depressions at equivalent points in previous long waves. The combined impact of these two powerful yet unavoidable forces is inescapable.

The stage is set for the collapse. In fact, some data suggest we are already on a bumpy downward decline similar to England's of the 1870s-1880s. Despite two sharp but brief recoveries in this decade's first half, industrial production is only marginally higher now than it was in 1979—the longest period since the 1930s depression in which production has not significantly exceeded its peak. Even following the severe 1973-1975 recession—the worst single cumulative decline in economic activity since the Depression—it took only three years for industrial production to significantly exceed its prerecession peak. This is a sign of a fundamental change in the economy's infrastructure.

The causes (and consequences) of this chronic economic malaise are threefold. First, business failures quadrupled from 1978 to 1982. Moreover, the expected mid-1980s recession and its aftermath could push failures 50% beyond the already-high 1982 level. Obviously, the absolute number of failures today is far larger than in the 1930s strictly because our economy is bigger, with many more participants than fifty years ago. Therefore, to compare business failures over longer periods it is better to convert the data to a failures rate. In 1978, the business failure rate was only 0.24% (24 failures out of every 10,000 businesses). Since it typically lags the economy by 6-12 months, and since the 1980 recession ended in July, by June 1981, the rate rose to nearly 0.61%—an indication that the nation's infrastructure was undergoing extreme changes which were significantly weakening the overall economy. And by the mid-1980s (the middle of another expected recession), the business failure rate could reach 1.26% and exceed 2.0% by the end of the decade. This compares to a 1932 peak of 1.54%, a post Korean War low of 0.24% in 1978, and a 1945-47 rate which hovered around 0%.

The second factor now readying us for the big fall is the speculative burst in oil prices—now primed for another collapse once the lagged impact of the mid-1980s recession is felt. The two earlier rounds of oil price declines have already resulted in two waves of the international debt crisis, threatening the very solvency of major worldwide financial institutions. If any one of the four or five most heavily indebted nations defaults on its debts, then—under current laws—major banks would be forced to recognize huge losses exceeding their capital, a situation which is tantamount to instant and massive failures.

Already, extensive loan losses from the 1981-82 recession are creating a surge in problem banks as defined by the Federal Deposit Insurance Corporation (FDIC). By September 1983, problem banks amounted to 597 banks or 4% of the nation's total banks, up nearly 55% from the previous peak of 385 or 2.6% in November 1976 following the 1973-1975 recession. Given the right spark, such a shaky financial system can quickly transform apparently placid investors and savers into panic.

The third megaproblem confronting the U.S. economy is the condition of the housing market. Simply put, Americans are losing the wealth they have in their homes. Although the effective price declines are often disguised by discount financing schemes, recent home sellers are finding their equity is not as large as they thought and are forced to help the buyers through special financing plans if the property is to be sold. Since consumers have locked up the bulk of their savings in their homes, overt or covert declines in middle-class home prices represent a major erosion of consumer wealth, which will at some point lead to a massive cutback in consumer spending.

These three factors—now poised to push the U.S. into a depression—are precipitated by the long wave's money/inflation paradox. The Federal Reserve maintains high real interest rates by gradually reducing money growth over a long timeframe. But despite the attempt at gradualism, this slowdown is traumatic for a country that needs ever larger doses of money just to keep economic activity from declining. Like a heroin junky addicted to three shots a week, reducing the intake to only two causes drastic withdrawal symptoms. Nevertheless, in order to eventually defeat inflation, such withdrawal pains are unavoidable.

Each of the economic scenarios reviewed in this chapter is guided by the overriding view that: (1) the U.S. economy is in the downward leg of a long-term growth cycle; (2) the next major event in our current long wave is a partial or thorough cleansing of the massive debt overhang; (3) no matter what policy options are chosen at this point, rapid real economic growth is not sustainable; and (4) that the economy is virtually on automatic pilot, forcing the hand of the Fed towards restrictive monetary policy and pushing the Government towards belated reversals of its overexpansive fiscal policy—just as occurred in the U.S.'s. 1920-30s and Britain's 1870-1880s.

The end result will be a depression which, to prevent, would require a massive issuance of money and a reigniting of inflation to such an extreme that a French 1790s or German 1922-23 type hyperinflation surfaces in the U.S. And just as those hyperinflations burnt themselves out once the middle class revolted in reaction to the destruction of their wealth, here too social and political pressure would force a return to disciplined monetary policies and precipitate the depression. Thus, even though widely varying assumptions are used, a depression develops in the 1980-1989 decade under any of the four scenarios discussed below.

The following forecasts were generated from a large mathematical model that evaluates the major interrelationships of the U.S. economy. Each significant economic function—such as consumer expenditures on goods and services and housing, business spending on plant, equipment and inventories, as well as various Government spending patterns—is represented as a mathematical equation. In total, the entire system includes 89 of these equations, consisting of a 32-equation weekly model—believed to be the only one of its kind—a 40-equation monthly model, and a 17-equation quarterly GNP model.

Unlike other mathematical systems, this one directly incorporates weekly and monthly data into the long-range projection. The mathematical model is a descendant from an earlier and much larger version that included over 450 equations. The underlying feature behind both the older and new versions is the synthesis of monetarist, Keynesian, and supply-side economic theories within the Kondratieff or long-wave cycle. Thus, these mathematical models duplicate the concept that each of the economic theories has its own time and place during different phases of the 40-60 long wave.

The four forecast scenarios can be split into two major types: (1) a 65% probability of a bona fide deflationary period from the outset and (2) a 35% probability inflationary acceleration creating a boom/bust period eventually ending in deflation. Two versions of each major type relate to their degree of severity. Each scenario is compared to the 1929-1933 U.S. depression and to the British 1873-1886 depression. To permit valid comparisons among these distant time periods, each is put on a standard basis. For each depression, many economic variables are referenced from the economic peak to the depression's trough or bottom. In most cases, the economic peak is used as the base from which cumulative percent changes are computed by year. The four scenarios are briefly highlighted below in order of their likelihood.

Four Scenarios

A. Most Likely Case:

International Debt Crisis Worsens As Oil Prices Collapse In Mid-1980s, Leading To More Severe Depression

—　　　Depression starts in the mid-1980s and reaches its bottom late in the decade. The most severe period of collapse is in the heart of the decade's second half.

—　　　The international debt crisis cannot be contained as a few of the most heavily indebted foreign nations default on their debt to avoid implementing further severe austerity programs at home. This results in bank and corporate failures unequaled since the last depression. The entire depressionary period is stretched out over a long expanse as compared to the U.S. 1929-33 experience, with a few very mild economic recoveries intermittently interspersed throughout the decade. Our mid-to-late 1980s depression more closely resembles the long British decline of 1873-1886 during which the percentage decline in production and other statistics is much less severe than that of the first-cycle depression. Actually the U.S. 1980s depression is about one-third the magnitude of the 1930s decline.

B. Most Likely Alternative Case:

Double-Digit Inflation As Fed Becomes Reluctant Lender Of Last Resort

—   Fed money pumping delays the start of the depression until later in the 1980s' second half. The most severe period of collapse is late in the decade.

—   Due to political pressure and fear of a widening of the international debt crisis, the Fed tries to boost money growth by a rapid 9% per year, temporarily delaying the depression until inflation becomes so severe that a return to slower money growth is demanded by the public. At the same time, the Fed becomes totally impotent to keep the economy from falling due to the total collapse in investor and consumer psychology. This lack of continual money pumping to feed the economy's addiction is a defacto Fed tightening which punctures the inflationary balloon and causes a depression. As before, the depressionary period is stretched out over a long time relative to the 1929-1933 collapse.

C. Second Most Likely Alternative Case:

Roller Coaster Depression As Further Worsening Of International Debt Crisis Is Averted

—   Depression starts in the mid-1980s as the full impact of the Fed's earlier switch to deflationary policies affects the overall economy, reaching its trough in the late 1980s. The most severe period of the collapse is midway through the second half of the 1980s.

—   The Federal Reserve gradually slows the amount of money pumped into the economy. As a result, the economy declines in fits and spasms punctuated at times by sharp, but brief, economic recoveries. Not only is the sharp plunge of 1929-1933 avoided, but the decline is also less severe than would be the case involving an international financial collapse. By various means the international debt crisis is patched up, containing its impact to that already experienced in 1982-83.

D. Least Likely Case:

Rampant Inflation As Fed Tries To Prevent Depression With All Its Power

— Political pressure becomes so severe the Fed tries to prevent a depression at any cost. Nevertheless the rampant inflation burns itself out in the mid-1980s resulting in a depression a few years hence. The most severe period of collapse is towards the end of the 1980s.

— To prevent the depression and an international financial collapse, the Fed pumps money into the economy at an accelerating rate as the decade proceeds. However, the Fed is unable to prevent the rapid transition from rampant inflation to depression. Even though this is much more dangerous than the others, it is still far removed in magnitude from the French and German hyperinflations. Consequently the U.S. social and economic fabric remains relatively intact, although severely weakened.

Most Likely Case—International Financial Collapse

In the most likely case, a depression evolves following the mid-1980s as the Fed continues to slow money growth in an erratic fashion. The key policy issue—both to the Federal Reserve and Administration—is the preservation of the Fed's hard-won creditability as a determined inflation fighter. But, as a result, the Fed alters interest rates to whatever level needed to offset the stimulative impact of the 1982 and 1983 tax cuts; this restrictive monetary policy neutralizes the expansionary fiscal policy; and Reaganomics fails to spur rapid, noninflationary growth.

Credit demands are consistently stronger than similar points in previous business cycles as businesses increasingly borrow to stay afloat or to maintain working capital. This stronger-than-normal credit growth, in turn, implies that money growth is also potentially stronger relative to similar periods in previous business cycles. Consequently the Fed is forced to maintain a more restrictive credit policy than in the past to prevent an acceleration in inflation. The end result is that the Fed is forced to bring about repeated recessions in order to keep money growth at an acceptably low rate. Meanwhile, banks are increasingly faced with large loan losses due to defaults by individuals, companies, or nations.

Thus, as typically occurs late in the long wave, reflecting the latent fear of an inflation explosion, real interest rates remain extremely high, shocking the already weakened economy to such a degree that a depression develops. Bear in mind that this sharp rise in real interest rates late in a long wave occurs even while nominal interest rates decline. This is because the Fed's strict monetary policy slows inflation faster than they are willing to let interest rates fall, causing the rise in real rates. Then, when actual deflation hits, real interest rates soar since nominal interest rates reach a rock bottom low level beyond which they cannot physically decline. The larger the decline in prices, the higher real interest rates jump.

The depression in a nation's first long wave of the supremacy cycle is marked by an immediate and mammoth plunge. In contrast, during the second long wave of the cycle, the slide into depression is usually split into two distinct phases: First a gradual downward move during which the economy's infrastructure is severely shaken despite the continuing increase in some economic numbers. Then, a brief respite is followed by a deeper plunge. Because the nation is more sophisticated, when the warning signs of another depression loom, the natural reaction is to prevent the onslaught. Simultaneously, previously instituted mechanisms to safeguard the system take some time to be chipped away.

In the U.S.'s second long wave of the supremacy cycle, the 1980-1983 period corresponds to the first phase. Take away the sharp recessions and recoveries during the past four years and you find industrial production has remained basically flat, while the unemployment rate rose by nearly 60%. For all intents and purposes, growth came to a halt. The economy became increasingly dependent on the service industries (such as banking, insurance, dining out, movies etc.) rather than manufacturing—another typical symptom of the second long wave as society attempts to smooth out the feasts and famines associated with the basic industries. Real GNP from 1970 to 1979 rose at an average annual rate of 3.1%, followed by a paltry 1.5% average from 1979-1983.

This economic stagnation is the gradual but painful transition from an inflationary to a deflationary bias in policy decision making—accommodating a restrictive monetary policy, causing a shift from low to high real interest rates. Inflation slowed dramatically. Year-over-year consumer price inflation, which was running at a 13-14% clip in 1980 and 1981, dropped to 4.0% by yearend 1983. In short, despite their erratic approach to the problem, the bottom-line results demonstrate that the Fed has indeed been following a deflationary policy since late 1979.

Other signs of the Fed's switch to a deflationary bias abound. Over the past three years, the two industries most responsible for the strong economy of the 1950s-1970s— housing and autos—suffered a massive, one-time drop to permanently lower sales levels: Housing activity of 1980-83 plunged 25.7% from its 1970s average and 31.2% from the 1977-79 period; total unit auto sales are off 14.9% from the 1970-79 average of 10.1 million to the 1980-83 level of 8.6 million; and, as a result of the decimation in these two sectors, basic industries like steel have fallen onto hard times also. In short, the smokestack sector which spearheaded our earlier long wave boom is in a clearcut decline, the ripple effects of which have caused unemployment to rise from 5.7% in mid-1979 to 8.2% in late 1983.

This period is also noted for its speculative binges, such as the stock market rally of mid-1982 to mid-1983, as forecasts of a dramatic turn for the better were repeatedly touted. However, with each passing day, the stock market should become more and more overvalued, given the horrendous earnings ahead and doubtful survivability of many companies in the mid-1980s. As the Fed continues to remain tough, the stock market should begin to drastically revise downward its earnings estimates, causing the overall market to tumble.

These trends are similar to Britain's depression 100 years ago—a transition period marked by a deterioration in basic industries during the early 1870s prior to the real drop from 1876 to 1886.[20] During this transition from 1872-1876, real incomes rose at only a +1.4% yearly rate down from a 5.6% average yearly rise in the previous five years; and prices fell 2.3% per year vs. an average yearly increase of 2.4% in the five years previous. In both Britain's transition phase of 100 years ago and our 1980-1983 period, a drastic slowing in real economic activity and a quick turnaround in price expectations wrecked havoc on businesses' ability to sell their products at a profit. Manufacturers saw their prices fall or not rise as fast, while their fixed overhead—acquired long before—was at a much higher cost. Thus, in both cases, the resulting profit squeeze forced large production cuts, bankruptcies, and a surge in the unemployment rate.

The depression takes shape in this decade's second half with the middle years being the worst in terms of the economy's rate of decline. An excessive debt overhang becomes too much for many firms to finance, leading to a rash of bankruptcies. The stock market continues to fall as investors recognize that many companies are not going to survive. The stock market plunge, in turn, causes a large decline in consumer spending, money growth, and overall economic activity. Since very few economic transactions are initiated, money growth contracts at an alarming rate. Governmental policies are ineffective in countering the credit collapse and the intense psychological fears that accompany the plunge.

A mid-1980s recession initiates the process towards an economic collapse. Although apparently "normal," the fact that it comes on the heels of two earlier recessions is its most noteworthy characteristic. This causes an overlapping of recession-related problems which, due to the brevity of the intermittent economic upturns, never get resolved, but rather pile up on top of one another, pushing the economy closer and closer to the precipice.

Currently, many individuals, companies, and nations are being kept alive through distress loans, as all hope the economic malaise is temporary. However, as it becomes increasingly apparent the economic situation will not improve and that the borrowers cannot keep up their debt payments after all, financial institutions and markets stop throwing good money after bad. New lending is halted and some existing loans are recalled. Investors lose confidence in the system.

Further compounding these woes is the sharply negative—but lagged—impact of the U.S. recession and strong U.S. dollar on the price of oil. As stated earlier, following the 1982 and 1983 oil price cuts, the Mexican and Brazilian debt crises emerged. The near-term solution has been to lend these nations more as they implement austerity programs which supposedly would later allow them to meet their debt payment schedules. However, these very same austerity programs, forced upon debtor nations by the international banks and by the International Monetary Fund, are causing severe political problems. Already many of these debt-laden nations are calling for debt repudiations rather than pushing themselves into an immediate depression as called for in the austerity program.

In this way, a drop in oil prices is the key to causing an unraveling of the international debt pyramid—by forcing most of the world's largest banks to write off loans that far exceed their available capital, by precipitating a major world banking collapse and, consequently, by causing consumer confidence or psychology to plunge. Needless to say, under these circumstances, consumer spending and the overall world economy spiral downward.

What is the likelihood of, and what would cause, another oil price drop? The current high U.S. dollar makes OPEC oil very expensive for foreign nations to buy, depressing oil demand as well as overall economic activity. This leads to less demand for U.S. goods also, causing a plunge in U.S. export sales (which happen to be overpriced relative to similar foreign products due to the strong dollar) and a major drag on total U.S. economic growth. This negative feedback effect of a high U.S. dollar plus the fact that the Fed is slowing money growth set the stage for a U.S. recession.

Extending all these interrelationships even further shows the drastic nature of the situation now developing. Since the U.S. economy is the locomotive for the entire world economy—impacting other nations about 6-12 months later—it can be thought of as tantamount to total world demand for oil. Since my mathematical model shows oil prices react to changes in the U.S. economic demand with a 9½ month lag, a sharp drop in oil prices should begin early in this decade's second half, all other things considered equal.

Even more important is the fact that the U.S. dollar negatively impacts oil prices with a long 1½ year delay. Since it has been hovering near its all-time high during much of 1983's second half, and since it was steadily rising for the nine months prior, the U.S. dollar's sharply negative impact also hits oil prices in the mid-1980s—roughly the same timeframe as the negative impacts of the U.S. recession. This "double whammy" implies a major oil price plunge—an oil shock causing an outright collapse in the debt pyramid with all its ramifications.

With both OPEC and non-OPEC nations already cheating on their production quotas to boost sagging revenues in the face of financial crises at home, the outlook is for even larger supplies at the very time the lagged impact of the U.S. dollar and economy cause demand to plummet. Consequently, oil prices should plunge from $29 to $20 during the mid-1980s and to a low of $10 late in this decade. The feedback from this oil plunge causes a domino effect of corporate and bank failures, leading to the most severe stage of the depression. Thus, the 1980s oil price collapse, in effect, corresponds to the 1929 stock market plunge.

During the true depressionary phase, real GNP drops a cumulative 9.6% from peak to trough, as compared to a 30.5% decline from 1929-1933. The S & P 500 stock price index plunges by 45.4% from 167.9 in September 1983 to 91.6 by the end of the decade, considerably less than the 73.4% crash of 1929-32.

The Fed funds rate (which is closely aligned to the 3-month Treasury bill rate) drops from over 10% in 1984 to 5% when the depression takes hold and finally to 3% by late in the decade (vs. the decline in short-term rates from 4.42% to 4.15% in the 1929-32 period and to 2.43% in 1946). But the sharp drop in nominal interest rates masks an even sharper rise in real interest rates as consumer prices decline a cumulative 26.6% during the decade's second half, similar to the 24.4% drop from 1929 to 1933. They key difference is that our 26.6% decline follows decades of accelerating inflation, whereas in the early 1930s it was preceded by a decade of deflation.

As businesses close at an alarming speed, the unemployment rate soars to 20.7% by the end of the decade. But although this appears to be comparable to the 25.2% peak of 1933, in actuality, it is not. Relatively few households had two wage earners in the 1930s, and less than one out of four working-age women were part of the labor force. In contrast, by late 1983, the female labor-force participation rate was 53.4%—more than double that of the 1930s. Thus, whereas unemployment of the household's sole wage earner in the 1930s was catastrophic, today if only one wage earner is unemployed, the situation is somewhat less desperate. The political, social, and psychological impact of 20%+ unemployment rates, however, is another matter entirely.

The other key difference between the 1980s and 1930s lies in the brief but feeble recoveries during the depressionary forecast horizon as policymakers try in vain to alter the events—short periods of growth which only temporarily halt the downward slide. However, the drawn-out nature of the collapse saps the nation's vitality, preventing a more thorough cleansing, weakening the foundation for the next long wave and, ultimately, jeopardizing America's preeminence as the dominant world power.

Again, the scenario duplicates that of Britain a century ago. Stop-and-go money pumping and bureaucratic institutions produced a lengthy British depression, interrupted by brief periods of recovery just as depicted for the 1980s. The unemployment rate, roughly 1½% before their depression, rose to 3½% by 1876 and soared to 10 3/4% by 1879, followed by a drop to 2½% by 1882. But from 1882 to 1886 the rate roared back to nearly 10% and averaged a hefty 8% during the 1884-1886 period. Consumer prices declined an average 1.2% per year from 1876 to 1886. And production of consumer goods fell approximately 9% during the worst phase of the downturn from 1874-1879—roughly equivalent to the expected production decline in the U.S. 1980s depression.

The First Alternative—Double-Digit Inflation

The first alternative scenario assumes an easier Fed monetary policy is instituted prior to the 1984 Presidential election. Since 1980-1983 economic growth is so weak, political pressures call for much faster economic activity by sharply boosting money growth and pushing interest rates down significantly. However, efforts to reflate the economy unleash an inflationary surge of such proportions that the Fed is forced to put a stop to it midway through the decade's second half. Although it is assumed in this scenario that the Fed supplies more money during the initial period than ever before—at a 9% annual rate—the very fact that they fail to increase the rate of high money infusion eventually puts a damper on economic growth, a problem typical of the latter stages of a long wave. Thus, the economy is in need of an even bigger money fix to keep it from sinking into depression. But because inflation has accelerated to such an intolerable level by that time, the Fed, the financial markets, the nation's creditors, political authorities, and the electorate are unwilling to

CHART 5.1. INDUSTRIAL PRODUCTION— THREE DEPRESSIONS COMPARED

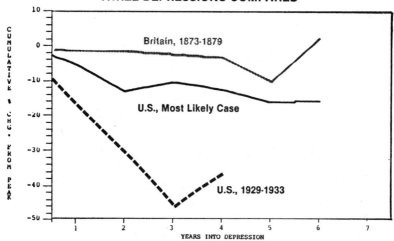

The 1980s depression will be somewhat steeper than that of Britain of 1873-1879, an equivalent stage in England's world supremacy cycle as compared to our current situation. In contrast, the 1930s collapse was much sharper since it was America's first depression within the 150-year supremacy cycle— a time when inexperience leads to sharp economic plunges.

CHART 5.2. UNEMPLOYMENT RATE— THREE DEPRESSIONS COMPARED

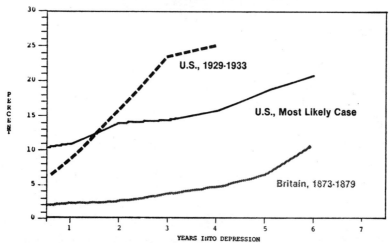

Although this decade's economic decline is to be less severe than the Great Depression, the unemployment rate will still rise above 20%, due to demographic and technological changes which are boosting unemployment over time. But, because of unemployment benefits and the prevalence of two-wage-earner families today, a 20% unemployment rate now does not imply the same degree of economic hardship as experienced 50 years ago.

CHART 5.3. CONSUMER PRICE INFLATION—
THREE DEPRESSIONS COMPARED

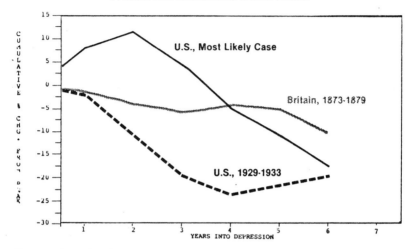

Because the 1980s depression will not be as steep as the 1930s collapse, the success in reducing the consumer price level will be limited. In addition, our deflation will follow years of massive price increases, whereas the Great Depression was preceded by a decade of falling prices—another sign that deeply imbedded inflationary pressures will return once the depression is over.

CHART 5.4. LONG-TERM INTEREST RATES—
THREE DEPRESSIONS COMPARED

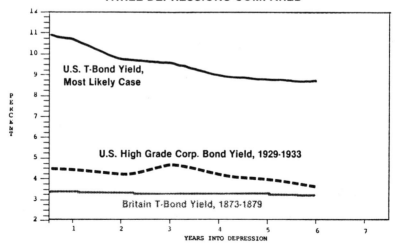

Due to our many years of rapid inflation and continuing budget deficit woes, long-term interest rates are to remain at a very high level. Going into the 1990s, high long-term rates will impede our economic recovery and world leadership position relative to others.

let it proceed any further. The depression—which should, by rights, have begun earlier—is finally allowed to take place.

A major possibility within the context of this alternative is that the monetary authorities and/or financial markets do not allow the reflation process to proceed for more than 6-12 months, much as we saw in 1979, 1980, and 1981. Prior to 1979, the Fed allowed money growth to accelerate from the early 1950s to late 1970s, culminating in year-over-year consumer price inflation of 12.8% by late 1979 and headed still higher, as compared to the 2.2% average inflation in the 1950s-60s. Thus, even though the nation was on the eve of a Presidential election, the Fed allowed interest rates to soar to record heights in early 1980, imposed credit controls, deliberately precipitated a six-month recession and, in general, began to institute the Draconian steps that led to the 1980-1983 economic quagmire.

The lesson was that an inflation rise to the low double-digit range was enough to enlist political and public support for anti-inflationary policies; and when inflation heated up shortly thereafter, the Fed again allowed interest rates to rise in late 1980 and in mid-1981 to choke off rising inflationary expectations. Each time, it took a somewhat lower year-over-year consumer price inflation rate to trigger the Fed's harsh response. Consumer prices were rising at a 12.8% year-over-year rate when the Fed altered its policy to a deflationary bias in late 1979, at 12.5% in late 1980, and at 10-11% in mid-1981 when interest rates rose to record highs.

Under this double-digit inflation scenario, year-over-year consumer price inflation reaches 10-11% (the Fed's previous last point of no further tolerance) by the mid-1980s and 12½ - 13% a year later. But by failing to increase their annual rate of money infusion beyond 9%, the Fed in effect calls a halt to the reflation, setting into motion the processes which lead to a depressionary phase beginning midway through the decade's second half.

The financial markets are another powerful force that can halt the reflation process long before it gets out of hand. In a knee-jerk reaction to the massive interest rate decline in mid-

1980, the economy soon perked up in 1980's second half. Gold soared to record levels, OPEC engineered further sharp oil price increases. And consumer prices were rising at a double-digit annual rate by late 1980 and early 1981—all despite the sharpest plunge in real GNP since the Korean War, a 9% decline in 1980's second quarter. In response to double-digit inflation, investors demanded higher inflation premiums in interest rates as the bond market itself forced interest rates higher. Given the severity of the situation, the Fed had no choice but to follow suit and boost the Fed funds rate from 9% in July 1980 to 19% in January 1981. Again, the lesson is that the financial markets may not allow the double-digit inflation process to get out of hand, implying that this alternative scenario could, in actuality, be much shorter than depicted here.

Once the depression does set in, however, it does so with a vengeance. Real GNP drops 13.6%. The unemployment rate soars above 20%, as in the previous case. And prices drop 30.5%—a larger decline than projected under the most likely assumptions, but also one which starts from a much higher base.

The Second Alternative—Roller Coaster Depression

The Fed's deflationary policy should cause the 1982-1983 international debt crisis to blow wide open. However, for argument's sake, the second alternative assumes that the international financial collapse is averted, and that the financial system somehow limps along.

When oil prices plunge in the mid-1980s, the IMF, Congress, Administration, foreign central banks, and the private banks contrive various measures to prevent the collapse of the world's largest financial institutions. Although foreign debt-ridden countries such as Mexico, Brazil, Argentina and other Latin American countries, as well as Poland and other Eastern Bloc nations, do in effect default on their debts, they do not officially announce a debt repudiation; and to prevent the ripple effects of this process, the debts are extended over a much longer time frame. In addition, all agree to delay the renewing of principal and interest payments to ten or more years down the road, allowing the nations to avoid the politically and economically devastating austerity programs.

Although the IMF's severe austerity solution may be the best for all in the long run because of its thorough housecleaning impact worldwide, it becomes politically infeasible. However, when it comes to their goals of preventing a depression, the IMF plan is as ineffective as the FDIC in preventing massive bank failures. The IMF instructs each troubled nation to import less and export more. But if the debt crisis is worldwide, how can all of the many countries in trouble increase their exports when their trading partners, also in the same group of debtor nations, are being told to restrict their imports? Obviously, if everyone is importing less then, by definition, they also must be exporting less, reducing worldwide economic growth.

As oil prices plunge in the mid-1980s, to forestall the consequences of the IMF-type approach to the galloping debt crisis, laws are changed so that the world's largest banks do not have to write off the foreign loans. If the bank loan defaults are recognized and the resulting losses are recorded on the income statement, these banks would not have sufficient capital to remain in operation—i.e., a bank failure. By changing the laws and extending the loans, these problems can be averted, technically speaking that is.

Another important requirement to avert the crisis is to convince investors and depositors that the banks are getting something in return for the foreign loans, such as equity in the assets of debtor countries or stock in the companies that are recipients of the foreign loans. As long as investors and depositors believe the worldwide economy and, by extension, these foreign companies, will eventually return to prosperity, then they may hold on in the hope that their money is secure in the long run. This scenario, however, assumes the foreign nations are desirous of solving the debt problem by eventually paying back the loans. In the event that (1) the foreign company goes bankrupt or (2) the foreign Government nationalizes the company and reneges on the commitment to the banks, then the entire "package" would be threatened.

Most crucial of all, a worldwide financial collapse can not be avoided unless consumer and depositor confidence is restored and maintained to such a point that a run on the banks never materializes. Otherwise, the various schemes to avoid recognizing the loan losses are meaningless and the withdrawals create a self-fulfilling prophecy, causing the banks to collapse and precipitating a domino effect for the international financial system. With plunging worldwide economies, an oil price collapse, stock market crashes, and the resulting loss of wealth worldwide, what would make individuals and businesses keep their funds—desperately needed just to meet cash flow commitments—in financial institutions, particularly in those with foreign loan problems? Clearly, under such uncertainty, the only rational choice for the individual depositor is to take his money now and ask questions later. In sum, this scenario has a relatively low probability because it seems highly unlikely that depositors could be convinced their funds are safe in the world banking system.

Third Alternative—Rampant Inflation

In the final economic scenario discussed for the 1980s, the Fed tries to avert a depression at all costs, flooding the economy with liquidity and pushing interest rates down sharply. Economic activity picks up dramatically so that a mid-1980s recession is averted, but to generate such an economic surge, money growth must continually accelerate.

Back in the Kennedy/Johnson era, money growth had to accelerate from an average of 2.6% per year in the three years prior to the 1964 tax cut to an average of 4.3% in the next three years in order to promote a sharp recovery. In contrast, in this third alternative scenario, money growth must accelerate from a 7.7% average yearly increase in the 1980-1983 period to 10% in 1984, 11% in 1985, 12% in 1986 and on and on—merely to prevent the depression's onset. The inflationary consequences are blatantly obvious.

The scenario begins with a money surge to avert (1) a mid-1980s recession, (2) the sure-to-follow oil price plunge, and (3) the collapse of the worldwide financial system. Normally, rapid money growth would lead to a stronger economy in roughly 6 months, and accelerating inflation with about a 1½ year delay. But as these events begin to unfold early in this decade's second half, the financial markets are unlikely to be fooled for long. Too many money and bond market participants are too wise to the inflationary implications and, within a very short time period (possibly 3-6 months), they begin to boost interest rates to reflect higher inflation premiums.

This forces the Fed to pump money into the economy at an even faster clip—first, to avert the short-term interest rate rise and, second, to push them down further. Inflation and inflationary expectations explode. Gold soars to an all-time high as consumer price inflation rises from 3.4% in 1983 to 14.4% in the mid-1980s. The vicious circle—between investors' boosting inflation premiums and the Fed's pumping an ever increasing amount of money to counter the natural upward pressures on interest rates—continues to accelerate during the next few years. But it finally collapses midway through the decade's second half when the Fed's ability to spur the economy any further dwindles to virtually zero; when the new money pumped into the economy—rather than being used for the purchase of goods and services—is converted almost instantly into inflation. The depression occurs in a furious downward spiral through the late 1980s.

Why Hyperinflation Is Unlikely in the 1980s

The probability of a U.S. hyperinflation in the 1980s is

dered low. In looking at past hyperinflationary periods—
_ _ _ _ as France in the 1790s and Germany in the 1920s—five
necessary factors are found, many of which are not present
now.

In any hyperinflationary period, the public and Governmental authorities need a viable excuse for firing the inflationary
coals; and a war or revolution in which the nation's very survival is threatened is sufficient. France ran up a huge deficit
to support the American Revolution and to thwart their archenemy, England, while, at the same time, feeding royal extravagances. But France did not try to increase taxes
sufficiently to offset these huge guns-and-butter deficits. With
the country in financial ruin by the late 1790s "... the financially beleaguered crown suddenly proclaimed that 'there will
be a temporary suspension of interest payments' on outstanding notes issued by the government."[16] This marked the onset
of a long process that precipitated the French Revolution and
a 25-year war with Austria. In short, the overlapping of these
monumental threats to both the Government and the aristocracy triggered the unlimited money creation as their last-ditch
attempt to cling to power and build wealth.

For Germany, the initial call to inflation was also in reaction
to a war. But in this case, the causes stemmed from the unrealistic reparations demanded by the allies for damages rendered during World War I—payments which were so large
that massive amounts of paper had to be printed to meet them
along with domestic needs.

In both the French and German hyperinflations, however,
much more than war, revolution, or their aftermaths were
needed to trigger the resulting hyperinflationary spiral. The
second most important factor was the lack of separation of
powers and the loss of checks and balances that such separation ensures. In the case of France, once the economic crisis
usurped the monarchy's power, the legislative branch took full
control of monetary decisions and issued fiat money in unlimited quantity to meet the Government's bills. In Germany, a
similar situation developed although the sole power resided in

TABLE 5.1
Requirements For Hyperinflation

---

1. Major war or revolution and its aftermath.

2. Nonexistent or limited separation of powers among the executive, legislative, judicial, and monetary functions of Government. No checks and balances. Control of monetary policy by sole seat of power.

3. Controlled State (i.e. monarchy or not truly developed democracy); suppressed public opinion.

4. Establishment of a deliberate Government policy in support of hyperinflation. This could be either:

    (a) For the benefit of a select few in Government and industry to profit handsomely from the hyperinflation; or

    (b) To prop up the economy after a war to prevent the normal postwar economic downturn which might threaten national defense.

5. Highly imbedded inflationary pressures in the third long wave of the supremacy cycle when the world leader is already weakened; intense international tension and competition for world supremacy.

---

the Monarchy rather than the legislature, as the Kaiser's absolute power carried over into fiscal and monetary matters. Without checks and balances, both these Governments were relatively free to follow hyperinflationary policies.

Furthermore, the public—normally the only remaining force which might be able to stop the hyperinflation process—had no voice in events. Thus, the lack of democratic institutions seems to be the third prerequisite for hyperinflation. In France, an authoritarian legislature sought to resolve the financial chaos with lies, trickery, and any other means at their disposal to keep the printing presses rolling. And in Weimar Germany, the public was also effectively prevented from impacting policy decisions.

With the absolute power to print money vested in the hands of few, Government policy could be altered to perpetuate the hyperinflation, to build the wealth of the minority in power, or simply to ensure that the minority stayed in power. This is the fourth prerequisite. In Germany, Government leaders and savvy industrialists viewed hyperinflation as a vehicle for the accumulation of personal fortunes; and in France those in power used the printing presses to maintain their power rather than implement unpopular corrective measures such as tax increases. Thus, in total contrast to the normal Government measures to cope with financial duress, the hyperinflation process becomes the sole power in and of itself. Everything is done to perpetuate it.

The last prerequisite for a severe hyperinflationary period is that it develops in the aging world power's third (and final) long wave of its supremacy cycle. France, although technically at the tail end of its second long wave, was already seeing the pressures that usually develop later in the third long wave of the supremacy cycle, whereas 1920s Germany was vying for England's supremacy position in Britain's third long wave, showing that it is the extreme political and economic tensions of this phase that are conducive to desperate acts to gain or maintain supremacy.

Is the U.S. likely to see hyperinflation during the 1980s? One can analyze the five prerequisites for hyperinflation in reference to today's situation. And, for confirmation, the factors that stopped the double-digit inflation during the Civil War, short of the totally destructive French and German versions, are also examined.

The U.S. did experience a brief rampant inflationary period during the Civil War. However, unlike the French and German versions, it never developed to the extent that the underlying social and economic fabric of the nation was radically rearranged. The capitalistic democracy that was developing prior to the Civil War emerged from the inflation spurt with all institutions intact.

The Civil War is analyzed in relation to the five prerequisites for hyperinflation in an effort to isolate those factors that stopped it short of the destructive French and German varieties. The first prerequisite—a war environment—was obviously met; and it was the need to fund the Union's war effort that justified an initial massive money surge. Because it was war, conditions were present to precipitate the second and third requirements. Under Lincoln's direction, the executive was indeed strengthened. The nation became a rather controlled state as our democratic functions were temporarily suspended. As the inflation advanced in its late stages in 1865, money pumping became a policy to maintain Governmental power and the wealth of the Northern industrialists. Not one of the power groups had either the willingness or reason to shut off the printing presses. Only the last prerequisite for hyperinflation was not initially met. The timing of the Civil War fell in the middle (i.e., the second long wave) of England's economic supremacy cycle.

Several critical facets of the American system appear to have choked off the development of hyperinflation. The major ones were the Civil War's end, the resumption of separation of powers, the reemergence of a democratic state, and the fact that the world leader at the time was not in the third long wave of its supremacy cycle. Moreover, upon return to peace, an economic decline ensued which brought the inflation to a halt. Unlike the German hyperinflation experience, which was rationalized as an effort to prevent an economic collapse following WWI, there were no external pressures to artificially sustain the economy—either to support a strong national defense or maintain a world empire—pressures which are typically present during the third long wave of the supremacy cycle. Meanwhile, internally, the prompt return to clearcut separation of powers, along with a resumption of public inputs, also served to end the hyperinflation. The only U.S. experience with potential hyperinflation as an industrialized nation demonstrates that the U.S. political mechanism, if operative, can be successful in halting it in the second long wave of the supremacy cycle. A question to be addressed later, however, is whether the U.S. system can prevent hyperinflation during its third long wave when the pressures for such a development magnify enormously.

Regarding the likelihood of a hyperinflation occurring during the 1980s, the previous example of the U.S. Civil War already suggests it cannot occur today without an obvious catalyst such as a war or revolution; and without the initial springboard to justify a money explosion, hyperinflation is even less likely. Moreover, a powerful new element has entered the picture to bolster the public's impact on Government policy in general, and an inflationary policy in particular; the bond markets have emerged as an anti-inflation pressure group with pervasive and continual influence on the political economy. To bond owners—as well as to lenders in general—inflation is a disaster that threatens to destroy the market value of their assets, quickly leading them to demand a higher inflation premium in their yield. Due to this new sensitivity, it took only 12.8% inflation in 1979 and 10-11% in 1981 for the Federal Reserve, with support from both the Government and the public, to tighten up on money.

Throughout 1978-81, inflationary policies led to a bond market drop and a U.S. dollar collapse, both of which periodically forced Governmental authorities back to a restrictive monetary policy as the Fed induced two back-to-back recessions during the 1980-82 period. Without a well developed bond market, the oil and stock market speculations of the 1970-1980s would have been strong public inducements to hyperinflation. With the bond market as an effective counter to these pressures, it is the deflationary forces which are prevailing. This is quite a contrast to earlier eras when inflation benefited the investment or speculative markets. Thus, not only has the U.S. system developed a strong Governmental defense mechanism against inflation, but it has also evolved sophisticated market mechanisms bringing instant, computerized feedback to Government actions, adding a new dimension to the public's role in preventing hyperinflation.

The final reason for not anticipating hyperinflation in the 1980s lies in the fact that the U.S. is still in its second long wave of the supremacy cycle. The pressures that build in the third long wave to make hyperinflation a real possibility are simply not yet present.

Forecast Summary

Under either a deflationary or inflationary scenario, a depression cannot be prevented indefinitely and any effort to do so—by trying to alter the natural flow of the long wave—can not remain effective for very long. In the most likely case of a sharp decline beginning around the mid-1980s, and in the second alternative, bringing instead a roller coaster decline, the depression—although still not recognized as such—is already in its preliminary stages. The depression takes place in this decade's second half, with the middle years of that period bringing the most acute and sustained period of turmoil. Under the less likely inflation scenarios, the actual depression is averted until later in this decade, at which time the plunge begins in earnest.

Although the 1980s will be very painful, the period does not last forever. In the 1990s the next long wave begins with an upward trend in economic activity. However, as Chapter 7 reveals, the 1990s-2030s long wave in no way duplicates America's glorious political power and economic growth of the past half century.

6

How to Escape the 1980s Financially Intact

If a depression is to develop, what should the individual, company, U.S. Governmental units, and foreign counterparts do to protect themselves from the financial ruin that will pervade much of the developed and developing world? This chapter discusses those economic sectors of greatest risk and greatest reward given the most likely scenario above. Individuals, companies, and Governments can then devise strategies to avoid the pitfalls that multiply dramatically during the next several years.

Before proceeding further, it is critical to point out that a very small minority of participants can profit significantly from a depression, while the majority is financially and/or emotionally destroyed. The following recommendations emphasize how to keep what you have; the first priority is to ensure that you at least walk away from the depression with no less than what you had going into it. By merely staying even (in nominal terms, without regard to deflation) your cash wealth relative to the rest of the population expands enormously. By accomplishing no more than avoiding losses, you can enter the elite class which has first access to special opportunities once the dust settles.

The key reason is deflation. Your constant or unchanged savings buy more goods and services than the same amount could prior to the depression. It is in this way, the very safes way, that the small saver or investor can profit after the depression. Most of us are not wheeler-dealers. Yes, a depression can be a period when great fortunes are made; but to do so can involve equally great risks, with a wrong move in such a treacherous period bringing devastating results. Fifty years later you only hear about the rare successes—not the multitude of failures.

Advice For Individuals

For the past several decades, the inflation beast has taught individuals to seek quick ways to maximize profit. What may be difficult for many to accept is that now you do not want to maximize your return by acquiring high interest bearing investments or by leveraging yourself with debt—both implying greater risk. Going into and through a depression, the last thing you want to do is incur risk unless you are an astute trader who is familiar with short selling. Do not worry that your 3-month Treasury bill rate is dropping. Do not be tempted by a municipal bond that yields much more. Chances are that municipal bond will default. Then your maximum return becomes a maximum loss. Upon maturity you know the principal on your Treasury security will be paid. No other medium of investment offers this guarantee. So all savings should be divided among direct investment in Treasury securities bought directly from the Fed, and/or nonbank money market funds that only invest in short-term Treasury securities, plus some cash.

These cash and highly liquid assets are the most valuable resources in a depression—for emergencies which will undoubtedly occur throughout its duration, for unexpected events bound to occur despite the best of planning or forecasting, and to give you quick access to your liquid funds with the assurance that your principal is secure.

It is the idea of absolutely ensuring the liquidity of your portfolio that calls for the investment in 3-month Treasury bills rather than the longer-term Treasury notes or bonds. In the early stages of a financial collapse, a rash of corporate loan defaults occur. Individuals with savings in banks withdraw their money in fear of a bank collapse. To meet the deposit withdrawals during this crisis, banks unload their investment portfolios, pushing the prices of Treasury notes and bonds down sharply. If you had a bond and were forced to sell it at this stage to obtain cash for an unexpected development, your capital loss could be severe. But the degree of principal loss narrows to practically zero, the shorter the maturity of the investment. So not only does a 3-month Treasury bill offer security and quick maturity, it also provides the lowest risk of principal loss if you want to sell it before it matures. The next best savings vehicle is a nonbank money market mutual fund that only invests in short-term U.S. Treasury bills. Because banks and other private financial institutions can and will fail, and because it is impossible to know which ones will survive, you do not want to hold deposits of any kind with them. Prudence, under such circumstances, dictates staying away from banks and thrift institutions altogether until the shakeout is clearly over.

For those individuals needing to ensure a specific level of income, the buying of Treasury notes now and locking in their relatively high yield is a necessity. However, those that do so must be assured in their own minds that they will not need to sell those notes when the economic upheaval develops. If you were forced to sell even risk-free Treasury notes during such financial turbulence, a potentially large capital loss might be incurred. So T-note purchases should only be with funds that are not to be touched for 5-10 years and done so only with the intent of receiving high stable income to meet expenses.

Since a maximum return is not sought during the depressionary period, there is no reason to incur debt. In fact, debt becomes a large negative drain on your cash flow once deflation sets in. Debt servicing at past higher rates saps your funds. And even variable rate debts will be a burden due to a considerable time lag in the interest rate decline relative to sharp declines in income. Therefore, under no circumstances should one be in debt going into a depression.

This means that, ideally, you should sell your home (even if it is at a loss) and rent until the deflation period ends. Those with debt will more than likely lose the asset anyway as the individual is unable to meet the interest and principal payments. Jobs and incomes—whether in upper or lower echelon positions—are reduced sharply during this period. Having debt and losing a job just compounds the financial and emotional woes, and involves the spectre of losing everything. Although the bankruptcy laws are liberalized now so that you can keep most of your assets even while claiming bankruptcy, don't expect these same laws to be in effect when the depression hits. The financial community will pressure Congress to pass tougher legislation to protect those banks that survive the initial shakeout. In short, to prevent financial ruin one must be out of debt when the depression hits.

Obviously, loss of income (either by unemployment or by a forced reduction in hours worked and/or salary received) is the one factor that can throw all plans awry. Basically all industries registered employee declines during the 1929-1932 depression. Since real GNP fell 30.5% during that period as compared to the most likely case of a 9-10% drop during this decade's second half, the employment decline for any industry during the 1980s depression should also be—on average—only about one-third the magnitude. In general, the largest production declines are in the areas that produce the most expensive goods like houses, cars, appliances, furniture, and business plant and equipment, bringing the most severe unemployment in the manufacturing and construction industries.

The sectors that are the safest in which to work are the new technology industries, although those too will be adversely affected during the more severe phases. In the 1929-1932 era, it was the airline and broadcasting fields which were expanding rapidly from very low levels of employment. The problem, of course, is correctly picking the appropriate growth industry. Some possible examples could be companies in synthetic food development and processing, or artificial intelligence programming for computers, to mention only two.

Most analysts think the service industries—entertainment, medical services, and amusements—would do well in a depression as people either need entertainment outlets to raise their spirits or require certain necessary services such as medical aid regardless of good or bad times. But in actuality, the service sector as a whole reduces employees in line with the national average. The only difference is that layoffs tend to come later in the depression than earlier.

However, there are notable standouts, or at least that was the case in the 1929-1932 period. The legal and educational service fields actually rose in employment, while repair and business service trades showed far smaller cumulative declines relative to the national and service industry averages. However, in the 1980-1989 period, the legal and educational areas are not likely to fair as well due to the relatively large supply of individuals already overcrowding these fields. Nevertheless, one would expect a surge in personal and corporate bankruptcy litigation, mergers, and divorces due to financial problems—all of which increase the demand for these particular legal services.

The Government sectors showed large employment increases during the 1930s depression. However, in the 1980s, Government jobs are not expected to be as safe. With massive deficits projected at all levels of Government, the pressure will be to cut staff. Whereas Government was viewed as an aid to stopping the 1930s decline, many will blame the huge Government payroll and deficits as a major factor behind the 1980s calamity. Despite these problems, political pressure to bolster the economy implies the Government sector will still be a relatively less dangerous place to work than most other areas.

Even if an individual is fortunate enough to retain his or her job, the probability of a cut in gross pay is high. Businesses can reduce total payroll expenditures through layoffs, by reducing hours worked, eliminating benefits or, cutting actual wages. Therefore, those individuals who continue on the payroll will—more likely than not—see their gross pay lowered. During the 1930s depression, amusement and recreation services (excluding motion pictures), educational services, utilities, banking, and the-then-upstart communication industry appear to have recorded the smallest gross pay reductions per employee. In contrast, agriculture, real estate and other construction, mining, and manufacturing recorded the largest losses. In general terms, the results will probably be similar in the 1980s.

Thus, recommendations for individuals during a depression are quite straightforward. Consumers should eliminate all debt now and build cash or liquid savings (i.e. 3-month Treasury bills or nonbank money market mutual funds investing solely in Treasury bills) by as much as possible, particularly for those individuals in industries where a high risk of being laid off is present. Expenses should be cut by as much as possible to boost cash reserves. If absolutely necessary purchases of appliances or properties are contemplated, try to rent if the option is available. As deflation continues, rents continually fall. But if you purchase a car or whatever, then you lock yourself into payments for what could soon become a grossly overpriced item. Until the economy starts to recover, do not even consider investments such as stocks, gold, silver, other commodities, CDs, corporate or municipal bonds, jewelry, art, stamps, or any other speculative items.

By following these suggestions, you escape the depression under less duress than you would have otherwise. And compared to others, you are in an enviable position. If your cash reserves are sufficient, once the depression reaches bottom and deflation stops, you can start to profit from your actions. Now your money can buy much more than it could before. Since it would have been prudent to rent your dwelling as mentioned above, you can now buy a house at a bargain price. The same obviously applies to other articles such as furniture, cars, etc. As to investments, once inflation begins anew, most long-term investments and speculative hedges such as stocks, gold, or commodities should become profitable once again.

Advice for Businesses

Much as in the 1929-1932 period, when virtually every conceivable industry grouping was in the red, substantial losses will be unavoidable during much of the decade's second half. Budget planning should be made accordingly. To prepare for the plunge in revenues, aggressive steps such as the elimination of all questionable product or service lines and an across-the-board reduction of staff levels are mandatory and should already be in place. The 1980s are a time for hatchetmen to reign supreme.

From the perspective of those living in the early 1980s, such steps might appear excessive or totally unwarranted. But when looking back at this period from the vantage point of the 1990s, it will be obvious that the depression was actually simmering in the first years of the decade; that we had already entered the pre-depression era. It is for this reason that selling your nonproductive assets is not easy, probably resulting in capital losses. Be that as it may, it is far better to minimize your loss now rather than incur a far larger loss later.

Thus, recommendations for businesses during the depression are similar to those for individuals. Debts—serviced at past high interest rates which destroy the income statement—must be eliminated and net equity built up. Plant and equipment must be rented rather than purchased whenever possible, allowing you to trade down to a lower cost item rather than being locked in at a high price.

The inherent problem for companies during the depression is that they are squeezed between falling revenues and high fixed expenses which must continue to be paid despite declining prices. To avoid this squeeze, variable costs should represent the highest proportion possible of total expenses; cash as a percentage of assets should be as high as possible; and external sources should not be relied upon for working capital. With banks and companies failing left and right, the likelihood of your enterprise obtaining an emergency loan is very dim. You must be able to survive by your own resources—not someone else's.

One way to prepare for this situation is to assume that the cumulative 26.6% price drop in the "most likely case" scenario is roughly representative of the expected revenue loss which, on a yearly basis, would come to an average decline of 7.4%. Second, evaluate your operations under this scenario to determine what must be cut to minimize losses or to turn a profit, enacting whatever proposals are drawn up to the degree feasible at this stage. Third, map out a worst-case scenario wherein revenues fall by double the amount expected in the most-likely case. Finally, plan all your actions around this latter scenario, which as explained in Chapter 7, is more than just a possibility.

For those in high-risk industries, the message is that expense cutting and product reviews should be instituted well before the depression hits, if there is to be any hope of averting the negative profit implications. These will be in the same general industry categories that suffered the largest sales declines during the 1930s—big-ticket items such as real estate, autos, appliances, furniture, jewelry, and business plant and equipment, all of which plunged much further than the overall average. Consequently, industries with the biggest profit losses tended to be durable goods manufacturers, whereas standout performers were banks, insurance companies, utilities, and food related industries. However, in the 1980s the banking and insurance companies will most likely come under greater profit pressure due to financial deregulation.

7

Will the U.S. Lose World Supremacy in the 21st Century?

With the 1980s depression leaving in its wake a bitter after-taste, a disbelieving public and bewildered Government, the dream-shattered nation begins the third long wave of her supremacy cycle in the 1990s. Just as the loss of the Titanic taught the world that an unsinkable ship cannot be built, politicians, economists, and the public will have belatedly realized that depressions are inevitable nightmares reappearing with frightening regularity. The once-heralded postulate that "the depression-beast is dead" is itself killed by the 1980s collapse.

America's ability to influence world events was beginning to subside in the 1970s due to the post-Vietnam paralysis that befell U.S. foreign policy and the post-Watergate paralysis that diluted the power of the Presidency. This is the tendency of an aging world power. In our case, the Vietnam ghost is eternally resurrected hampering most military initiatives. In an analogy to the Fed's economic impotency, the U.S. Government's political and military machinery are weakened as most U.S. actions are hampered by fervent public attacks, self doubts, and internal debate.

The stagnation that hits our political and foreign policy

institutions also strikes at the very core of the nation's economic potential. Unlike countries such as Japan, West Germany, China, and Russia, U.S. economic growth is hampered by our inability to fully eradicate the excesses that should have been erased in the 1980s depression. Although the depression acts to temporarily cool the fires of inflation, deeply imbedded inflationary expectations remain high. Simultaneously, the probable initiation of National Health Care, social security payments from general revenue funds, and other publicly demanded social programs—along with a need to fortify our military defenses against ever-menacing outside threats—drain the resources available for launching a powerful economic recovery.

With many near-bankrupt or Chapter 11 companies avoiding the more thorough liquidation process implied by Chapter 7-type bankruptcy and therefore still in operation during the 1990s, venture capital needed to bring new innovative processes to the forefront is nowhere near as prevalent as following the 1930s depression. And without a strong technological base to efficiently and inexpensively produce our products, other nations increasingly outsell U.S. goods and services. In short, our deeply imbedded inflation puts our products at a severe disadvantage during the next long wave—a trend which is countered by a raft of trade protectionist legislation. But it is no more than a crutch to offset the real, underlying problems of an inflation-drained superpower.

Very similar conditions prevailed in Spain, France, and England during the third long wave of their supremacy cycles. Each past world economic leader became complacent towards rapidly changing events, relying instead on past successes. Each was slow to adopt the new long wave's most innovative processes, dooming it to a game of catch-up throughout the third long wave. The failure to eradicate the inflation-nemesis during the previous depression blocks the aging power from regaining her supremacy.

For example, English production growth during the early phase of the 1890-1939 recovery was sharp. But unfortunately for Britain, other nations—quicker to implement innovations—benefited from lower inflation and had fewer demands for Government-assisted social programs to heal the major wounds of the past depression. Consequently, Britain lost her earlier competitive advantage, and English production growth was far short of the explosive rise experienced by other more vibrant economies coming out of the 1880s depression. A similar pattern surfaces in the U.S.'s 1990-2030 long wave.

With the weakening of our political and economic power base during the 1970s and into the 21st century, America faces increasingly aggressive challenges to her supremacy as the third long wave unfolds. The frightening question is: What occurs during the third decade's major war? It is this war that historically precipitates the dethroning of the world leader by a new one. By the time of a nation's third depression as a world leader, the mantle of world economic and political supremacy has historically been shifted to another. Although later in this chapter ways to minimize or prevent our loss of world supremacy are identified, the next several sections assume the supremacy cycle is once again repeated, to America's detriment.

The Fate of Previous World Leaders

If it is our destiny to relinquish control of our world preeminence, then what is to happen to us as nation? This is a very emotional and controversial question. Yet, it is of the utmost importance that it be asked in order to isolate and understand what actions might now be needed to avert or alter the currently expected outcome. Will the world leadership transfer to an ally such as Australia, Canada, Japan, or West Germany? Or will it fall into the hands of a foe such as Russia? The last transference of power was between allies, with the U.S. gaining world supremacy over Britain in the early 1900s; and subsequently, the U.S. safeguarded Britain's institutions and way of life from German aggression in both World

Wars. But in most previous cycles, the transference occurred between enemies.

The differences or similarities between the British/U.S. transference of power on the one hand and the earlier Spanish or French cycles on the other should provide some clues as to our nation's fate. When the British defeated Napoleon at Waterloo, they had no intention of invading France or conquering the world. Nevertheless, Britain did indeed rise to world supremacy by defeating Napoleon and, in most cases, became a defender of other nations' right to peaceful existence. Since France was evolving into a more capitalistic or free-market nation, it was to Britain's best advantage to enter into peaceful trading relations with France as well as other nations. The wars that Britain fought were primarily to counteract the aggressions by other nations or to open once restricted markets to British trade. Moreover, these battles were in remote territories which were no threat to the past world economic leader—France.

Thus, the British rise to power mirrored very much the subsequent U.S. emergence as a world leader. The U.S. also used trade with previous foes in addition to the united efforts by our allies to institute democracies and maintain worldwide peace. Like Britain, the U.S. found the expansion of foreign commerce to be a greater source of wealth than actual occupation of the previous leader.

The French and Spanish, however, were not so kind to the previous world leaders. Spain's influence was destroyed by the French in the War of Spanish Succession as the French actually tried to take outright control. The combined efforts of other lesser European powers, such as England and Germany, countered France's efforts to occupy Spain but, despite this setback, France was unquestionably the dominant power.

Spain became, in effect, a French satellite and the leash was tight enough to drain her of valuable colonial possessions, reducing Spain to a backward, third-rate nation. Then, in France's third long wave of her supremacy cycle, she did briefly invade Spain, until British and allied forces liberated her from French control, later defeating Napoleon. Similarly, 100 years earlier, just prior to Spain's first 50-year period of its supremacy cycle, the Spanish invaded Portugal, the previous world power, with the Spanish rule over Portugal continuing for half a century. Thus, French and Spanish supremacy cycles were very damaging to the previous world leader's existence as an independent nation.

Upon reviewing these historical examples, several patterns can be gleaned concerning the deposed world leader's dependence or independence under the dominance of the new world leader. If the new world leader is free trade or market oriented, then the old world power becomes a valued ally. Increasing trade— rather than invasion and occupation—is a far better course economically and politically for both countries. The transfer of power from Britain to the U.S. is a prime example. If, however, the new world economic leader is dictatorial, desirous of empire building, a natural philosophical or religious enemy, and/or not a free trade advocate, then the old world leader can expect an invasion attempt. Both the Spanish and French supremacy cycles displayed these characteristics and, partially as a result, their supremacy cycles lacked the financial and political strength observed in the British and U.S. cycles where wealth accumulation through trade was more prevalent.

Whether or not the old world leader remains independent depends on the abilities and desires of other world powers to come to its defense. In the Spanish cycle, Portugal was occupied for nearly sixty years before any other nation could successfully intervene; whereas in the French cycle, other world powers quickly came to Spain's aid, moderating to some degree France's domination of the Spanish.

Who's Next In Line?

When the U.S. draws closer to the third decade of her third long wave of the supremacy cycle, the question will become:

Will the U.S.'s successor as world economic leader be a friend or foe? To answer this question, one must determine the degree to which the factors that preceded the world supremacy cycles of Spain, France, England, and the U.S. can be observed among today's potential candidates for world leadership. As noted earlier, there are six prerequisites that must be met in the long waves that precede a nation's rise to world supremacy.

Following the supremacy cycle's dating scheme, one nation should possess the characteristics necessary to raise it to world economic and political supremacy over the U.S. within 20-40 years. Historically such power transference has occurred during the third decade's major war, or 2010-2019 in our third long wave of our supremacy cycle. However, in view of the holocaust which would result from a nuclear conflict, the transfer of power— if it occurs—is not expected to entail a war directly between the U.S. and the newly emerging power. Instead, the transference of power is likely to occur through indirect wars causing U.S. economic stagnation relative to others as the aging U.S. industrial machine encourages more frequent indirect attacks. Who are the most likely prospects? The most likely potential candidates include Australia, Canada, Japan, West Germany, China, and Russia. Table 7.2 summarizes to what degree each contender currently meets the preliminary requirements to be the world economic and political leader.

In reviewing Table 7.2, Canada, which intuitively would rate very high as a potential future world leader, has many internal divisions which have yet to be resolved. The continual issue of Quebec's secession from the Union must be resolved before Canada can hope to push forward. And a common failing of all Western industrialized nations is the lack of extensive land acquisitions which would have generated the advanced and efficient military complex needed to be the world leader. Over the next 30 years, Canada can be expected to make headway in resolving its internal difficulties, but not to the degree necessary to make it the world leader.

TABLE 7.1
Prerequisites For World Leadership

---

1. Elimination of any direct foreign influences on the homeland (i.e. revolution if necessary).

2. Civil wars to solidify domestic priorities in the direction of the industrialists and against the agriculturalists. Thorough modernization of industrial base to efficiently outproduce competitors and to build the most successful military war machine possible.

3. Agricultural self-sufficiency.

4. Nation isolated geographically, politically, and economically allowing development to occur without much outside interference.

5. Extensive land aquisitions to widen sphere of influence, gain access to needed resources, and once again promote self-sufficiency to as much a degree as possible. Way to train and fine-tune military efficiency.

6. Adopting an increasingly free-trade or capitalistic orientation with the concurrent easing of constraints on individual rights.

West Germany and Japan are also unlikely to evolve into the next world economic supremacy position. For both nations, elimination of direct foreign influence and the presence of a solid domestic front are not currently observed for similar reasons. Since World War II, West Germany and Japan have been precluded by international law to maintain anything but a defensive military force. In addition, these two countries have seen the most well orchestrated anti-military movements. To be a world leader these nations would have to resolve both the international laws precluding them from offensive weapons and develop strong public support for the military complex. As Table 7.3 later shows, international pressures do not allow the resurrection of the World War II axis powers.

The next 3 potential candidates—i.e. China, Australia, and the Soviet Union—have relatively high chances of becoming

TABLE 7.2

Present Condition: Are Preliminary Requirements Met To be World

Economic and Political Leader?

	Australia	Canada	Japan	West Germany	China	Soviet Union
1. Elimination of Any Direct Foreign Influences.	Yes	No	No	No	Yes	Yes
2. Civil War— Industrialization	Yes	Yes	Yes	Yes	Partial	Yes
3. Agricultural Self-Sufficiency	Yes	Yes	Yes	No	No	No
4. Nation Isolated Geographically, Politically, and Economically	Yes	No	No	No	Yes	Yes
5. Extensive Land Acquisition or Colonization - Fine-Tuned Efficiency and Strong Military Complex Supported by Public	No	No	No	No	No	Yes
6. Increasingly Free Trade Oriented	Yes	Yes	Yes	Yes	Partially	No
Total "Yes" Answers	5	3	3	2	3	4

the next world economic leader since the lacking requirements appear easier to acquire than those for West Germany, Japan, and Canada.

China, although a power to reckon with in the future, has too many problems to be resolved over the next 30 or so years to allow it to obtain world supremacy. Although they are striving to make the necessary corrections now, one senses that their intent is with defensive rather than offensive motives, particularly vis-a-vis the Soviets which are feared intently. Thus, China's fairly rapid modernization program may be keyed to a strong defense before their well-oiled offensive powers are pursued. What China currently lacks is the industrial complex which is a necessary prelude to agricultural self-sufficiency and the development of a modern military machine. In recent years they have put into effect partial free trade policies to steer actions more aggressively toward rapid industrialization. But the sheer magnitude of their population makes this goal a lofty one to achieve. Their time could be 150 years later.

Although Russia does not currently have the highest score as the most likely candidate, she, nevertheless, is in the best position to rectify her problems prior to the next long wave's third decade. Obviously the Soviet Union has the backing of its people for maintenance of a strong and efficient military. Russia's sphere of influence is worldwide. Yet few efforts are made to counteract any of her attempts at further colonization as exemplified by the attack of Afghanistan, considered outside the realm of influence of the Western powers. This is the mark of a nation that is in the prime position to build its power base with relatively little intervention. In addition, indirect influence is being achieved covertly through surrogates such as Cuba, Vietnam, and most recently, Nicaragua—a powerful long-term plan towards dominance of key world areas. Having learned to avoid direct contact with the Western military machine, and by gradually and subversively gaining control, they have been able to wear down the Western powers' will and ability to counteract their moves.

What stands in Russia's way to becoming the world economic and political leader within 30 years? The number one obstacle is the total lack of free trade or capitalistic-type incentives to spur agricultural self-sufficiency. This implies their industrialization process is also lacking similar incentives to generate a highly efficient and innovative industrial complex. With each successive world power developing a strong free-enterprise economy, it forces a contender to make similar strides if it has any hope of economically overwhelming the power that quickly emanates from the capitalistic approach. The communist philosophy precluding these capitalistic tendencies would therefore seem to prevent Russia from ever acquiring the necessary pillars of support to launch a world supremacy campaign.

However, the Soviets could conceivably overcome this obstacle in two ways, and there is evidence they are indeed moving in that direction—a fact which should be noted with great alarm by the U.S. and all Western industrialized powers. First, Russia can undertake direct and indirect measures via colonization to first surround, and then block off, new markets to prevent a further feeding or injection of vitality into our capitalistic economic development. To steadily grow, the capitalist system must have ever-expanding markets to nurture and harvest. Without the incentives of new markets to explore and sell to, the capitalistic economy stagnates, evolving into an increasingly socialistic society. Secondly, the Soviets are seeking to increasingly introduce capitalist-type incentives in the agricultural and industrial sectors to boost production and reduce dependence on Western grain and technology. Both of these solutions are discussed in greater detail below.

In Table 7.2, Australia currently rates the highest of any nation by virtue of its five qualifications for supremacy. However, Australia's one missing element happens to be the most difficult to put in place. Like all Western nations except the U.S., a large, strong, and effective military complex is not established.

Australia's lack of colonization is not really a constraint since all Western industrialized nations could unite behind a free-trade oriented Australia which could effectively substitute for a large and independent colonization program. When times are rough, these nations are closely knit. When times are free of major pressures, each may act as a sibling bickering among one another; but upon the slightest threat to any one member, trade and political ties quickly draw them back together. Nevertheless, by not developing a colonization program, Australia has lost the opportunity to build and fine tune its industrial and military machine.

The Soviet Union is implementing a two-pronged strategy which makes her the most likely candidate for the next world political and economic leader. First, their apparent long-term goal of surrounding capitalistic nations and choking off new markets is in perfect agreement with their Marxist dogma. They recognize that trade is the lifeblood of a capitalist nation; and that by shutting off potential markets, they can back into world supremacy by watching the Western industrialized nations gradually fall into decay and internal unrest. Thus, under this strategy, the capitalist system is like a medieval castle under siege—surrounded and starved by the lack of economic opportunities. They also realize that if they fail in this effort and Western nations do find new markets, it would bring such a strong shot-in-the-arm that Russia might be unable to offset the economic surge. So, second, to counter this possibility, the Russians are also endeavoring to acquire economic wealth by increasingly employing capitalistic techniques in agriculture and industry.

Heretofore, the Russians have primarily tended to take a pure Marxist approach to the free-trade and agricultural self-sufficiency problems. Marx had expected capitalist nations to fall once their markets were saturated with products. What he failed to see—but what Kondratieff did see—was the ability of the capitalist society to resurrect itself through innovations and applying them to new markets. Thus, contrary to Marx's expectation, a depression did not bring on the downfall of capitalism, but rather set the stage for its next major upward surge. Therefore, Russia initially resorted to their preferred choice of stopping capitalism by cutting off all new markets, causing the slow strangulation of the capitalist system.

To date, however, two major areas for capitalistic expansion appear to be opening which are increasingly threatening

Russia's long-range goals. The first is America's commercial and military applications of the space shuttle, giving Western nations a big head start towards future space colonization. Developing innovative and cheap production processes in space should yield new products and greater profits for Western nations even if additional markets on earth are shut off. Aware of this potential, Russia can be expected to push much more aggressively towards military space supremacy and space industrial research. The second major area for capitalist expansion is the opening of China to Western trade—a process which is already underway to some extent.

The weakness of the traditional Marxist strategy to slowing or stopping capitalist development is that it takes a considerable amount of time and resources to implement. So another solution is also being implemented by the Soviet Union which allows them to take advantage of the U.S.'s increasing impotency during the third long wave of the supremacy cycle.

The second approach is to employ capitalistic techniques and incentives in agriculture and industry. In this way Russia controls its own destiny and can determine the appropriate timing for seeking the world mantle. The pure Marxist approach makes Soviet policy dependent on the actions of the West. Although the implementation of free trade practices initially seems farfetched, Russian leadership has already shown clear signs of being more pragmatic, in contrast to the more dogmatic approach earlier in the 1900s. They have increasingly experimented with such incentives; and, over the next 30 years, one can expect them to dramatically expedite this process. Western nations should remain on the alert for this development, for it is the missing link in the Soviet drive for world economic and political domination.

Intuitively, it may seem unlikely that Russian authorities would ever allow the extent of reforms necessary, but such changes are already surfacing within the Soviet empire. In Soviet Bloc nations such as Hungary and Poland some very advanced capitalistic practices are being encouraged, and a concurrent small shift towards greater individual freedoms is being permitted. These appear to be serving—intentionally or not— as test sites, helping Moscow determine the best vehicles for implementing similar changes in Russian society. An acceleration of this trend can be expected over the next 30 years making Russia the only contender to successfully meet the requirements for world economic supremacy.

Table 7.3. summarizes the expected situation around 2010-2019, the time of the U.S.'s third decade during its third long wave. Historically, this point in time results in the transference of world economic and political supremacy to another nation, sometimes a friend, sometimes a foe. Based on trends in progress today and the cycles that have been discussed in depth, the most likely outcome 30-40 years hence is for the Soviet Union, an obvious foe, to replace the U.S. as the world's dominant economic and political force in world affairs. Of all the Western nations, only Australia seems potentially capable of countering Russia's attempt to be the next world economic leader. But, whereas Russia can resolve her remaining problems independently—and, more importantly, already appears to be doing so—Australia would need special aid and considerable prodding to become the U.S. heir-apparent,an unlikely outcome which opens the door for Russia's power drive.

The Threat of Hyperinflation in the 21st Century

In addition to the question of our nation's security in the third long wave of our supremacy cycle, there is also a great risk of an economic and social catastrophe through hyperinflation. As detailed earlier, there are five factors that appear necessary to precipitate a hyperinflationary spiral. The first requirement—war—would be met, by definition, within the third decade. And, with the third long wave of the supremacy cycle being in operation, the fifth requirement for hyperinflation is also met. Meanwhile, the combination of these two—the extreme pressures of war and the nature of the third long wave itself—could easily blur the separation of

TABLE 7.3

Future Conditions: Will Preliminary Requirements Be Met By Early

21st Century To Be World Economic and Political Leader

(Assuming Continuation of Present Trends)?

	Australia	Canada	Japan	West Germany	China	Russia
1. Elimination of Any Direct Foreign Influences.	Yes	Partial	No	No	Yes	Yes
2. Civil War - Industrialization	Yes	Yes	Yes	Yes	Yes	Yes
3. Agricultural Self-Sufficiency	Yes	Yes	Yes	No	No	Yes
4. Nation Isolated Geographically, Politically, and Economically	Yes	No	No	No	Yes	Yes
5. Extensive Land Acquisition or Colonization: Fine-Tuned Efficiency and Strong Military Complex	No	No	No	No	Par-tial	Yes
6. Increasingly Free Trade Oriented	Yes	Yes	Yes	Yes	Yes	Yes
Total "Yes" Answers	5	4½	3	2	4½	6

powers (the second requirement) and the ability of the public to voice its opinion (the third requirement) should the President invoke emergency war powers as occurred during our Civil War.

Only the fourth prerequisite—the idea that hyperinflation

must become an official Government policy—is not intuitively obvious. In earlier periods, it was a time for a select few to profit from the wealth that hyperinflation initially creates. But in this instance, rather than personal reward, the rationale for any hyperinflation (if it develops at all) would be to prevent the sharp economic plunge that follows the war. Such an economic downturn would probably be viewed as a threat to our national defense. Postwar public support and separation of powers might be repressed due to the Russian threat. The prevailing view may be that a postwar economic collapse must be prevented at all costs to defend our power and ward off Russia's growing strength.

Also, similar to Britain of the 1930s-1980s where their bond market ceased to function for all intents and purposes, our extremely strong inflationary tendencies later in the third long wave of our supremacy cycle will have destroyed the bond market as a viable force in the economy. Since the U.S. bond market is such a key aspect in preventing hyperinflation in the 1980s, this could be a major loss in trying to ward off hyperinflation during the next fifty years. The next section discusses ways to avoid hyperinflation and Russia's rise to power.

How To Retain World Leadership

The long wave cannot be prevented but, at a severe cost, Russia has shown that its timing and amplitude can be adapted and altered to a nation's long-term advantage. In Russia's case, the continual state of depression has worked to suppress free thought and allowed the Soviet leadership time to sharply cut the typical lead times required to rise from a third rate power to an industrial and military giant. Now the cycles imply Russia will relax these individual restraints to bring agricultural and industrial innovation up to Western standards. Evidence suggests Russia is doing just that, using her knowledge and unquestioned acceptance of these cycles to systematically put herself in the position to acquire world economic and political supremacy within the next fifty years.

Our challenge is to also accept and use these cycles to halt their advances and maintain world peace. Just as Russia has paid a heavy long-term cost with perpetual depressions, we too must accept sacrifices which will be no less hard to swallow.

Simply put, the U.S. and her allies must promote a 1980s depression of greater magnitude than the 1929-1933 slump, lasting perhaps 10-20 years. Only by so doing can capitalist nations rid themselves of the inefficient companies, huge debt overhangs, and to put aside the perpetual cheer-leading that "everything is or will soon be rosy." Such perpetual optimism has torpedoed each supreme power preceding us.

The U.S. and Western way of life is in grave jeopardy; and the complacent or disbelievers will merely cause history to repeat itself. Nothing in life is ever obtained without pain and hard work. Birth, growing up, love, learning a profession—all involve short-run pain to reap long-term benefits. The same philosophy must be followed, without hesitation, throughout the third wave of our supremacy cycle.

The following list identifies specific options, in order of preference, which are available to stop Russia's drive for power and to avoid hyperinflation. These options can be mutually exclusive or implemented concurrently. To be in the strongest position to ward off the Soviet Union and debilitating inflationary pressures, however, it is recommended that all options be followed with the utmost speed and united sense of urgency.

First, the U.S. extends its supremacy cycle into at least a fourth long wave by dismantling, now, the social safety nets designed to cushion any economic collapse. Policymakers then deliberately induce a 1980s depression of greater magnitude than the 1930s. The thorough housecleaning eliminates the deeply imbedded inflationary psychology, permitting significant innovations, a return to rapid economic growth, and maintenance of our political power following the depression. Other Western nations synchronize their economies with the U.S. depression to produce a large downturn for all.

As part of this process the Fed is given true independence—much like the Supreme Court—with a solid mandate to fight inflation. By this further separation of power, the U.S. economy is assured of avoiding the ultimate hyperinflationary debacle. The bond market remains a viable source for financial capital and an effective counter to unchecked speculative tendencies.

Upon coming out of the 1980s depression, the Western Alliance is in a position to out-innovate, out-produce, and out-maneuver the Soviets in hitting new markets. Since inflation fears are the biggest inhibitor of our future growth, deflation must be sharp and continue for a substantial period. Also, since the resulting debt crisis will paralyze many Latin American, Soviet Bloc, African, and Asian nations, the Western Alliance should be very selective as to whom we help return to prosperity. For example, we must let Russia draw down its reserves to bolster Soviet Bloc nations; while the West rebuilds those nations that are sure to be bulwarks against future Russian aggression.

Since there is no way to avoid the depression, it is better to have it sooner than later. Much like a toothache, the sooner it is remedied, the less pain that will be incurred in the long run. And the more radical the cutting of the fat, the leaner and meaner the U.S. and other Western nations can be in their duel against future Russian advances. By meeting strength with strength, future wars can be averted.

Second, Western nations should give significant aid and assistance to Australia to bring her along as the heir apparent to the U.S. This is a contingency plan if the U.S. electorate does not tolerate a deep depression. Australia, along with her Western allies, would be the center of strength to ward off Russian aggression.

Third, U.S., other Western nations, and China should act in unison to counteract future Soviet aggression and to open up new markets.

Fourth, the U.S., Western allies, and China should establish an all-out program to effectively utilize space for industrial and military purposes.

Fifth, nations should share in developing extremely advanced computer technology, particularly regarding artificial intelligence. Such technology will bolster our industrial potential and economic wealth during the third long wave, preventing Russia from acquiring an economic upper hand.

Sixth, Western nations should give significant aid and assistance to China to strengthen her industrial and agricultural base. Since China fears Russia as much as, if not more than, Western nations, such indirect protection against Russian attacks is a common goal.

Summary and Epilogue

The analysis of the Kondratieff wave and the world economic and political supremacy cycle must force American and free-thinking nations to a sense of urgency for long-term national survival. The double-barrel conclusions that (a) the world will experience a 1980s depression and (b) that this depression could be a prelude to Russia's attempt to seize world economic and political power, are bound to be controversial. But the very nature of that controversy puts into perspective the urgency for quick, forthright, and long-range decisions by the U.S. and our allies if we are to prevent these forecasts from coming true. Just as Russia is now using these cycles to map out a plan towards world supremacy, the Western industrialized nations and China can also use these same cycles to prevent Russia's rise.

A necessary prerequisite to stopping Russia's attempt, however, is the public's knowledge of these probable events and their total support in preventing Russia's plans for dominance. And, although the initial steps towards this end (involving a severe worldwide depression) are extremely harsh, they lay the groundwork for the dawn of a new age in technological advancements and united space exploration. Perhaps by showing our strength and determination, Russia will seek to be a friend rather than a foe, thus eliminating the war that normally develops in the third decade. Under such a united effort, the entire world political structure can proceed to greater achievements.

World peace can be preserved because of the universal awareness of precisely those aspects during the long cycles that lead to war. Quick recognition leads to quick prevention. But let there be discord within the Western Alliance over the next 30 or 50 years, and we will be gradually pulled into an age of totalitarian control.

The choice is ours. If we opt for inflation, we will have inadvertently created an insidious tool working in Russia's favor. If we opt for controlled deflation—the staunch defense of the integrity and buying power of our currencies—we will have chosen the proper capitalist response to this ultimate threat.

> Let this paper bring a resurgence of reality so that the final and ultimate calamity can be avoided. The hour is late indeed but unless the leadership of our country commence to realize they cannot legislate stability, that placing the yoke of oppression on their constituents while continuing to keep the power of the printing press, we will all go down the road to chaos. We must have a standard of value if we are to survive. The price to be paid at this late date will be severe, the major question is shall we be left with a currency or not.[20]

Appendix

The forecasts underlying this book are generated from a fully operational forecast system consisting of linked weekly, monthly, and quarterly econometric models of the U.S. economy. The Kondratieff cycle dominates long-run economic activity in all models, while money growth is the key variable in determining real GNP and inflation in the short run. The weekly model projects M-1 growth, interest rates, production, initial claims for unemployment benefits, stock prices, the trade-weighted U.S. dollar exchange rate, and more. The weekly model's short- and medium-term money supply, interest rate, and economic activity projections are directly incorporated into and constrain the monthly model. The monthly model forecasts key series which are later used to project real GNP components in the quarterly econometric model. The total system includes 89 equations consisting of a 32-equation weekly model, a 40-equation monthly economic model, and a 17-equation quarterly GNP model.

The system is constructed with two key aspects in mind. First, the long wave economic theory or Kondratieff cycle is implicitly built into the modeling system forcing the projection to conform to the latter stage of the Kondratieff cycle. And second, money growth and movements in real consumer wealth (i.e., primarily stock prices) are considered the main driving forces behind the economy in the short run. Monetary policy dominates fiscal policy—i.e. the Fed can neutralize fiscal policy actions, whereas the reverse is not true.

The theory and statistical background for the forecast system is presented in my two previous books. An earlier and much larger linked system of 450 equations is discussed in *Linked Weekly, Monthly, Quarterly Econometric Models of the U.S. Economy (Volume 1)*. And a related book reviews the smaller model used to generate this book's forecast. The second book on the modeling system itself is entitled *Condensed Weekly, Monthly, Quarterly Econometric Models of the U.S. Economy (Volume 2)*.

NOTES

1. Batten, Dallas S., "Inflation: The Cost-Push Myth." *Federal Reserve Bank of St. Louis Review.* June/July 1981, pp. 22, 25, 26.

2. Graham, Alan K., "Lessons from the 1920's for the Computer Industry: A Long-Wave Perspective for R & D Strategy." Alfred P. Sloan School of Management, MIT, Cambridge, Massachusetts. March, 1980, p. 10.

3. Stoken, Dick A, *Cycles: What They Are, What They Mean, How To Profit By Them.* The McGraw-Hill Book Company. 1978, p. 174.

4. Graham, op. cit., p. 10.

5. Ibid.

6. Ibid.

7. Panati, Charles, "Catastrophe Theory—A Framework for Analyzing Discontinuous Events." *Newsweek.* January 19, 1976. pp. 54-55.

8. Friedman, Milton and Anna J. Schwartz *A Monetary History of the United States, 1867—1960.* Princeton University Press, 1963. pp. 322, 324.

9. Mayer, Thomas, J.S. Dusenberry, and Robert Z. Aliber *Money, Banking, and the Economy.* W. W. Norton & Company, Inc., 1981. pp. 606-607.

10. Friedman, Milton and Anna J. Schwartz, *Monetary Trends in the United States and the United Kingdom.* The University of Chicago Press, 1982. p. 609.

11. Hamilton, Earl J., "The Decline of Spain." in *Essays in Economic History; Volume One.* E.M. Carus-Wilson, ed., Edward Arnold Publishers LTD., London, England, 1954,

p. 225.

12. Stoken, op. cit., p. 38.

13. Ward-Perkins, C. N., "The Commercial Crisis of 1847 " in *Essays in Economic History: Volume Three.* E. M. Carus-Wilson, ed., St. Martins Press, New York, 1966, pp. 263, 275.

14. Hamilton, op. cit., p. 226.

15. White, Andrew Dickson, *Fiat Money Inflation in France.* The Caxton Printers, LTD., Caldwell, Idaho, 1958, p. 9.

16. Tinbergen, *Business Cycles in the United Kingdom, 1870-1914.* North-Holland Publishing Company, Amsterdam, Netherlands, 1951, pp. 187-189.

17. Beales, H. L. "Great Depression˙ in Industry and Trade " in *Essays in Economic History: Volume One.* E. M. Carus-Wilson, ed., Edward Arnold Publishers LTD., London, England, 1954, pp. 407, 409.

18. Ibid, p. 412.

19. Bagwell, Philip S. and G. E. Mingay, *Britain and America . 1850-1939.* Praeger Publishers, New York, 1970, pp. 177-178.

20. A personal observation written by Donald Wilk on January 8, 1973 after reading Andrew Dickson White's *Fiat Money Inflation In France,* a history of the French 1780-1790s hyperinflation and subsequent political and economic ruin.

BIBLIOGRAPHY

Bagwell, Philip S. and G. E. Mingay, *Britain and America 1850- 1939*. Praeger Publishers, New York, 1970.

Batten, Dallas S., "Inflation: The Cost-Push Myth." *Federal Reserve Bank of St. Louis Review*. June/July, 1981, pp 30-26.

Friedman, Milton, *Dollars and Deficits*. Prentice-Hall, Inc, Englewood Cliffs, New Jersey, 1968.

Friedman, Milton, and Anna J. Schwartz, *A Monetary History of the United States, 1867-1960*. Princeton University Press, 1963.

Friedman, Milton, and Anna J. Schwartz, *Monetary Trends in the United States and the United Kingdom*. The University of Chicago Press, 1982.

Graham, Alan K.,"Lessons from the 1920's for the Computer Industry: A Long-Wave Perspective for R & D Strategy." Alfred P. Sloan School of Management, MIT, Cambridge, Massachusetts, March, 1980.

Graham, Frank D., "Hyperinflation: Germany, 1919-1923." in *Readings in Economics*. Paul A. Samuelson, John R. Coleman, and Felicity Skidmore, eds., McGraw Hill Book Company, New York, New York, 1955, pp 138-141.

Hamilton, Earl J., "The Decline of Spain " in *Essays in Economic History: Volume One*. E. M. Carus-Wilson, ed., Edward Arnold Publishers, LTD., London, England, 1954, pp 215-226.

Levy-Pascal, Ehud, "An Analysis of the Cyclical Dynamics of Industrialized Countries." Central Intelligence Agency, Directorate of Intellegence, Office of Political Research, January, 1976.

Mayer, Thomas, J. S. Dusenberry, and Robert Z. Aliber,

Money, Banking, and the Economy. W. W. Norton & Company, Inc., 1981.

Mingay, G. E., "The Agricultural Depression, 1730-1750." in *Essays in Economic History: Volume Two.* E. M. Carus-Wilson, ed., St. Martins Press, New York, 1966, pp 309-326.

National Income and Product Accounts of the United States, 1929-74. U. S. Department of Commerce.

Panati, Charles, "Catastrophe Theory—A Framework for Analyzing Discontinuous Events." *Newsweek,* January 19, 1976, pp 54-55.

Phillips, A. W., "The Relation Between Unemployment and the Rate of Change of Money Wage Rates in the United Kingdom, 1861- 1957 " in *Macroeconomic Readings.* John Lindauer, ed., The Free Press, New York, 1968, pp 107-119.

Schwartz, Anna, "Understanding 1929-1933 " in *The Great Depression Revisited.* Karl Brunner, Ed., Kluwer & Nijhoff Publishing, Boston, 1981, pp 5-48.

Shapiro, Max, *The Penniless Billionaires.* Truman Tulley Times Books, Quadrangle/The New York Times Book Company, Inc., New York, 1980.

Stoken, Dick A., *Cycles: What They Are, What They Mean, How to Profit by Them.* McGraw-Hill Book Company, 1978.

Tinbergen, *Business Cycles in the United Kingdom, 1870-1914.* North-Holland Publishing Company, Amsterdam, Netherlands, 1951.

Varian, Hal R., "Catastrophe Theory and the Business Cycle." *Economic Inquiry,* Vol XVII, January, 1979, pp 14-28.

Ward-Perkins, C. N., "The Commercial Crisis of 1847 " in *Essays in Economic History: Volume Three.* E. M. Carcus-Wilson, ed., St. Martins Press, New York, 1966, pp 263-279.

White, Andrew Dickson, *Fiat Money Inflation in France.* The Caxton Printers, LTD., Caldwell, Idaho, 1958.

Wolman, William, and Jeffrey Madrick, "The I.M.F.'s Perilous Plan for Growth." *N. Y. Times*, October 2, 1983, pp 1F, 8F, 9F.

Zambell, Richard G., *Linked Weekly, Monthly, Quarterly Econometric Models of the U.S. Economy (Volume 1)*. Weiss Research Inc., West Palm Beach, Florida, 1984.

Zambell, Richard G., *Condensed Weekly, Monthly, Quarterly Econometric Models of the U.S. Economy (Volume 2)*. Weiss Research, Inc., West Palm Beach, Florida, 1984.